C000144424

An A–Z of
Dressage
Terms

An A–Z of Dressage Terms

LÉONIE M. MARSHALL

J. A. Allen
London

British Library Cataloguing-in-Publication Data.
A catalogue record for this book is available from the British Library

ISBN 0.85131.633.6

First printed 1979
Reprinted 1987
Reprinted 1991
Revised edition 1996
Reprinted 2002

© Léonie Marshall, 1996

No part of this book may be reproduced, stored in a retrieval system, or
transmitted, in any form or by any means, electronic, mechanical,
photocopying, recording or otherwise, without the prior permission of
the publisher. All rights reserved.

Published in Great Britain in 1996 by
J. A. Allen & Company Limited,
1 Lower Grosvenor Place, Buckingham Palace Road,
London, SW1W 0EL

Typeset by Textype Typesetters, Cambridge
Printed by Midas Printing International Ltd. Hong Kong

Designed by Judy Linard

Contents

Above the bit

This is an evasion of the bit. It is recognised by the fact that the horse carries his head too high and cannot be easily controlled. Because the head is in the air with the nose well in front of the vertical the action of the bit is ineffective.

The horse will be unbalanced and will have a hollow back making it impossible for him to carry himself and his rider, except with extreme difficulty.

This evasion is a serious fault because it prevents the correct development of the muscles which will hinder the horse's progress. Until it is corrected, training cannot proceed.

CORRECTION
A horse which is above the bit has not been taught, or not understood, that when the rider takes a contact on his mouth, he must yield, not resist.

How does the horse learn to accept the bit? The answer to this is probably one of the most difficult things to explain because so much depends on the knowledge, feel and hands of the rider.

Theoretically, the rider closes his legs and feels the mouth evenly with both hands until the horse bends at the poll, relaxes his lower jaw and 'gives' to the hand. The rider then must instantly ease the pressure, but not so much that he loses what he has just achieved.

In practice, the procedure can be quite difficult unless the rider is sensitive and knows what he is doing. Much depends also on the type of mouth the horse has, unmade, made, or spoilt.

In the case of the made mouth, the matter is relatively

simple. The rider will close the legs and take up contact. The horse feeling this will bring his head into position with no resistance, and away they can go.

The unmade mouth causes a good deal of confusion amongst riders. Most riders are very much aware that any careless handling of their horse's mouth will cause callouses and in consequence, hardening. Therefore there is a great reluctance on the part of many riders to take much contact at all on the unmade mouth. Oddly enough although their motives are honourable, the result is not what they expect. Little or no contact, will never teach the horse to accept the bit. Only a firm or 'asking' hand, then easing and lightening of the contact when the horse has 'given' to the bit, will make him understand.

Many riders are insufficiently interested to make or improve a mouth, hence, there are many horses who have never been taught to accept the bit and have spoilt mouths. (A horse who is above the bit must be treated as having a spoilt mouth). These horses are a menace, they are resistant to the hands and often turn nappy when someone tries to insist on them doing something they do not want to do. With this lack of acceptance incorrect habits occur and many horses get a bad name, unfairly.

With knowledge and understanding these bad habits can be corrected but any retraining must necessarily take quite a long time because the horse must unlearn before he can relearn. (If nappiness has become confirmed the horse may never be completely corrected, although with patience and determination the situation can be improved.)

When there is a lot of resistance, as in the case of the spoilt mouth, the rider must, basically, apply the usual aids, taking a much firmer contact, slightly more leg and overcome the resistance until some relaxation occurs. The horse should be kept at a slow speed at first, preferably in walk, so that there is no extra impulsion to cope with. Maintaining a slow walk with a firm contact, the rider must make sure that the horse is going forwards. He must not keep a dead pull on the reins but must move the bit gently in the horse's mouth by squeezing one rein and then the other. As long as the reins are not loosened, after a period of time the horse will lower his head to a better position, the rider should then control this improved head position with a light contact. Most riders give up before this is achieved and the correction is never established. If the rider perseveres and the horse lowers his head, he should be rewarded with a pat on the neck.

All this may take several days because it should only be carried out for short periods each day (as long as it takes to achieve a result), but with patience the horse will ultimately learn to keep his head in the correct position.

Until the horse will accept the bit in walk, the trot should not be attempted.

Abrupt transition

A transition is a change from one gait to another, walk to trot, trot to canter etc. or, an alteration of stride within a gait. For example, collection to extension etc.

An abrupt transition usually occurs if the rider has given his aids too suddenly and without sufficient preparation. As a result, balance, rhythm, head carriage etc. may be lost.

CORRECTION
Throughout the training the rider should aim to make all transitions as smooth as possible. To achieve this, there are several factors the rider must take into consideration.

First, the rider must allow for the time lapse, however small, which occurs when his thoughts have to be transferred to his muscle system and, in turn, to the horse's brain and muscle system.

Secondly, the rider must prepare the horse and warn him that that something is going to happen. These warning aids are called half halts. Because the half halt is used so much in training, I have quoted the definition of the half halt as given in the B.H.S. Rules on Dressage, so that it is accurate.

11

The Half Halt

The half halt is a hardly visible, almost simultaneous, co-ordinated action of the seat, the legs and the hand of the rider with the object of increasing the attention and balance of the horse before the execution of several movements or transitions to lesser and higher gaits. In shifting slightly more weight onto the horse's quarters, the engagement of the hind legs and the balance on the haunches are facilitated, for the benefit of the lightness of the forehand and the horse's balance as a whole.

The half halts correctly used are of vital value in the training of the horse. In the early stages with the young horse the experienced rider uses the half halt in a very minor degree. It may be necessary to use them frequently to help the horse stay in balance and to improve the quality of the steps by making the rhythm constant.

Later, the hind legs may be brought more under the horse by slightly stronger aids, but only when the horse is physically ready to carry more weight on the hindquarters.

If the horse is correctly prepared for the transitions by the use of the half halts to maintain balance, and if there is no resistance to the hand, the rider should be able to take the horse smoothly from one gait to the other. Straightness must also be a vital factor.

Advancing

This comment is used during piaffe when the horse does not remain sufficiently on the spot.

CORRECTION
Suggestions for correction have been made on page 25 under *Creeping*.

Against the hand

Basically this term refers to a resistance to the hands of the rider, as opposed to a yielding.

CORRECTION
When the horse resists the rider's hands he is tensing his lower jaw in order to evade bit pressure. Only submission to the pressure can enable him to work properly. Submission can only take place as the result of engagement of the hindquarters, a rounded outline, suppleness and acceptance of the rider's leg and hand combined. If the horse will move forwards willingly from use of the rider's legs, he can then be made to be submissive in the jaw by a feel and ease action of the hands. The 'feel' or firm contact with the mouth is to ask the horse to yield to the bit, the 'ease', the reward for having done so. Easing, does not mean loosening the rein, but maintaining contact more lightly.

Angle varied or varying

This comment would be made usually during the shoulder-in and simply means that the angle is constantly altering.

CORRECTION
Angles vary mostly because there is insufficient impulsion or engagement to keep the horse forward to the control by the rider's hands. Asking for too much or too little angle and then trying to make an alteration can also be a cause. The aim should be to ask for and maintain an angle of 35 degrees with a true bend, good impulsion and submission.

Anticipated or anticipation

This occurs when the horse thinks he is aware of what is about to happen.

In the case of a transition the horse may try, or succeed in trying, to make the transition before the rider's aid.

CORRECTION

As it is a necessary part of the test for the horse to be obedient, he must learn to wait for the rider's aids. In training the rider must be careful that he is always in control of what is happening. The horse may not choose what he wants to do nor when, he must wait until he has a directive from his rider.

Some riders find it difficult to concentrate on the way their horses are going but they must choose whether they want an obedient horse or not. It is not fair to the horse to let him choose the gait sometimes and then expect him to be obedient to the rider in a test.

It may sound rather boring to have to teach the horse to be completely controlled but once the horse will wait for the aids he is a much easier and nicer ride.

Back not round

This expression is intended to indicate that the horse is not using his back correctly and instead of swinging it upwards towards the rider, he holds his back away, in a flat or hollow posture.

CORRECTION

If the horse is to be a comfortable ride and if he is to progress in his work he needs to be relaxed and supple in the back. The rider must be very aware that he is not sitting heavily in the saddle which will cause discomfort and eventual 'hardening' of the back muscles.

The only way that the horse's back will be comfortable to sit on, is if he is worked with his head and neck in a natural position without resistance and with his hind legs working actively under him. The rider must beware of the horse coming above the bit, or too high in his head carriage which will cause hollowing of the back. This also prevents the hind legs doing their job effectively.

It is unnecessary to allow the horse to put his head very low in order to get the back round, but the horse should offer to 'lower' if the rein is given. If he does not, it is doubtful if he is using his back correctly.

If the horse does not offer to lower when the rein is given, the rider may not have a good enough acceptance of the bit (see page 9). He should check on this aspect and also try changing gait several times, as this will make the horse use himself more. If he is working harder, he will be more likely to want to stretch his head and neck, which will in turn slightly stretch the back muscles.

Balance not maintained

This comment describes the state of the horse when he is either momentarily off balance, or if the balance is generally lacking.

Momentary loss of balance is not necessarily a great crime so long as the horse was balanced in the first place, but if the balance is lost for any length of time many things can go wrong. The horse will probably alter rhythm, be irregular in the stride, come off the bit, fall on the forehand, etc. All these problems will lose the rider many marks.

CORRECTION
Throughout the training of the horse, the rider must work for the perfection of the balance.

The first aim should be to try to put even weight, of both rider and horse, over the horse's four legs, so that no one pair of legs is being overworked.

Because the horse is naturally heavy in front owing to his head and neck, he may carry too much weight on the forehand. As he develops physically and strengthens, he must be asked to bring his hindquarters more under his body so that they eventually take more of his weight. The forehand will be lightened as a result.

It will be necessary to use steadying aids, constantly, to correct or assist the balance. These are generally called half halts (see page 12) and may be used in varying degrees. With the young horse these half halts consist of merely a slight slowing of the speed, with the rider making sure that the hind legs still work and do not become inactive.

The rider will want to maintain light leg aids so he may use the schooling whip to assist him. When applying the schooling whip, the hand should be kept on the rein, so as not to disturb the contact with the mouth.

As the training progresses, the degree of the half halt may be increased to transfer more weight to the hindquarters.

Behind the bit

This is an evasion, with the horse not accepting the bit. The horse draws back from the bit and will not allow a contact to be taken. The nose is usually behind the vertical which is incorrect.

CORRECTION
The rider should first check that the bit or bits fit correctly and that his horse's teeth are not catching on the bit and causing discomfort. He must check also that he is maintaining a satisfactory contact and that he has not caused the horse to come behind the bit by being heavy handed.

If the cause is not any of these things the rider should take an even contact with the horse's mouth and let him feel the hands. Then he should ask the horse to go forward first at a steady speed, but then increasing the activity to give the gait more impulsion. At the same time he should try to encourage the horse to bring his nose in front of the vertical by allowing with his hands any forward movement asked for by the horse.

Vary the gait from a shorter stride to a longer one until

there is sufficient energy going into the hand. When altering the gait, do not change speed but try to lengthen or shorten the stride in the same rhythm.

Behind the leg

This term means that the rider has failed to keep the horse sufficiently forward from the leg aids.

CORRECTION
At all times when the rider's leg aids are applied, the horse should respond at once. His failure to do so means they have not been taught properly to him. There are many moments in training when the horse is reluctant, confused, or merely lazy, but if he is to be successful in dressage competition he must be instantly obedient. The schooling whip may be used as an additional aid to achieve this if neccessary.

Behind the movement

This comment refers to the rider and means that the body of the rider is behind the vertical and he may be putting too much weight on the loins of the horse thus impeding the action of the hind legs and movement of the horse's back.

CORRECTION
When training the horse much concentration is directed at the way the horse is going, but the rider must constantly check his position because only the correct position will have the right influence on the way the horse is going.

Broke

This expression is used when the horse, of his own will,

changes the gait he is in to another. In other words if he is in canter and falls for a moment to trot and then back to canter, that is a break in the gait.

CORRECTION
With training, one of the most vital factors is the correct balance of the horse at all times. The rider must be very aware of this point and constantly try to ensure that he assists the horse as much as possible.

Breaks in the gait are usually caused by a loss of balance or possibly a mistaken aid. The rider must make sure the *speed* at which he is riding is not unbalancing the horse. Very often less experienced riders allow their horses to go too fast so that the horse cannot control his own weight; lack of balance must follow.

When the horse is properly balanced he can carry himself at any gait without falling out of it, with only light contact from the rider's hands and legs.

Half halts (see page 12) play a big part in balancing the gaits. The rider should also make sure that his aids are always clear so that the horse will not misunderstand and break the gait for this reason.

Broke rhythm

This term is used mostly during trot extensions and means that a momentary alteration of rhythm of the steps has occurred.

CORRECTION
The cause of breaks in rhythm can be poor ground, loss of balance, crookedness, resistance, stiffness or alteration of the rider's position. Good preparation for the movement and maintaining engagement of the hindquarters will help the horse to hold his rhythm and stride.

Canter broken

This remark I think, should mean that the three-time gait is not entirely true, but sometimes the comment may refer to a horse cantering croup high, which does give the impression of the horse cantering in two pieces, first the forehand and then the hindquarters.

CORRECTION
I believe the rider should first check that the gait is truly in three-time and that the balance (see page 15) is correct, then concentrate on the hindquarters and try to work the horse to improve the length of stride. This means using half halts and constantly correcting the rhythm and balance. Also, the canter may need to be more forward with a better movement of suspension between the strides. Variation in the gait, i.e. coming from working canter to a degree of collection and back to working, can help to improve the suspension.

Changed behind

This fault can occur during a canter pirouette owing to lack of balance or stiffness, it may also happen in canter when the hindquarters try to swing out, or in canter to trot transitions if the horse is not properly on the aids.

CORRECTION
In all canter work the horse should be slightly bent towards the leading leg, changing behind can only take place if the rider allows the hindquarters to escape the control of his outside leg or if he inadvertantly allows an alteration of the bend.

Changing rhythm

This comment refers to an alteration of the steps within a gait. Instead of moving with regular, steady strides, the horse, for one reason or another, breaks the length of the stride for one or more steps. This alters the rhythm.

CORRECTION
First of all check on the speed of the gait, and make sure that in no way is the horse unbalanced. Secondly, make certain that the horse is accepting the bit evenly on both sides of his mouth, by testing him with the hand. Squeeze a little first on one side and then on the other to make sure that the yield is equal. The rider must then concentrate on the rhythm he wants and, if it helps, count the footfalls.

In walk, the footfalls should be in four-time, each foot coming to the ground separately.

In trot, the rhythm is two-time, as the legs come to the ground diagonally. For example, the near fore and off hind, and then the off fore and near hind.

The canter is three-time. Leading with the near fore, for example, the horse will start with the off hind followed by the near hind and off fore, and then the near fore, followed by a moment of suspension.

Circle too large/small/square

A judge often has to deduct marks for incorrect size and shape of circles. This is rather a waste of marks so it is worth finding out how to ride the right size. (See Figs. 1–4.)

CORRECTION
Firstly, a circle must be round. The rider must try to visualise the circle on the ground and look ahead to see where he is going. Secondly, it helps some riders to aim at certain points on the circle to help to get them in the right

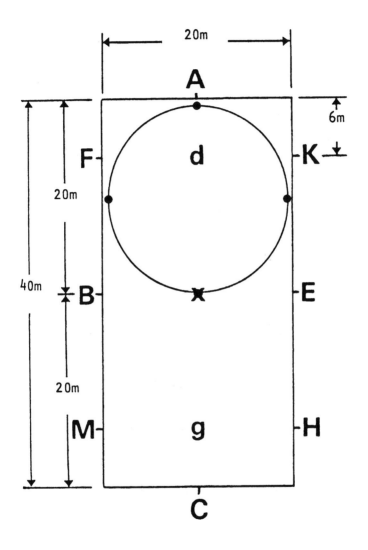

Fig. 1 Arena and 20 m diameter circle

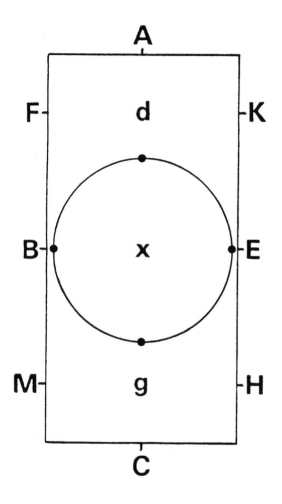

Fig. 2 Circle: 20 m in diameter

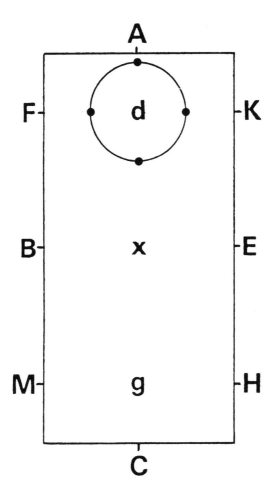

Fig. 3 Circle: 10 m in diameter

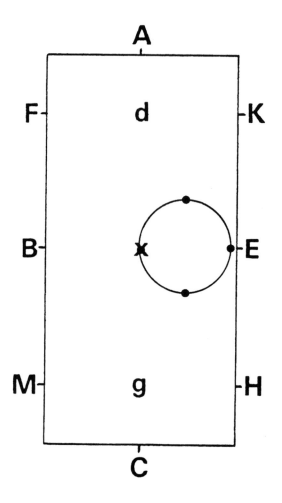

Fig. 4 Circle: 10 m in diameter

place. On a 20 m circle the rider should aim for the four points, as shown.

Having achieved the correct size circle, the rider must curve the horse to the shape of the circle and keep the bend constant. He should hold the horse to the circle with the outside rein, using the inside leg to keep the horse out and bent slightly. The inside rein may be used a little against the neck to work in conjunction with the outside rein and also create some flexion. The outside leg must control the hind-quarters and prevent them flying out.

The speed and rhythm of the gait must be steady and regular.

Creeping

This term can be used for two reasons. Firstly in walk when the horse is not going forwards properly, and secondly in piaffe when the horse is escaping forwards instead of remaining on the spot.

CORRECTION
Creeping in the walk is mainly the fault of the rider not the horse, because is it the result of overcareful or restrictive riding for one reason or another. It may be done to avoid jogging, breaks of rhythm, unlevelness or pacing. The horse is not truly on the aids or being ridden forwards in a rounded outline.

To avoid creeping in the piaffe, better collection and the use of many correctly ridden half halts will prevent the steps from gradually stealing away from the original place of asking.

Crooked

This term could be used at any time when the hind feet of the horse are not following the forefeet.

CORRECTION
To be able to ride straight, that is to say, with the horse's hind feet following in the same track as the forefeet is of prime importance at all times, and can only be achieved if the rider has the ability to use his aids evenly and effectively and can feel when there are deviations. During training there will be many occasions when the horse tries to use the weight of his shoulders to go where he wishes, or avoid the rider's legs by swinging his hindquarters. Stiffness can cause crookedness so suppling exercises should be practised equally on both reins. Some riders are slack about changing diagonals in trot when changing the rein, this will in time cause the horse to develop unevenly and may create crookedness.

Crooked halt

This means that the horse has stopped with his quarters to one side or the other of his forehand so that he is not straight.

CORRECTION
A crooked halt is often caused by resistance to the hand so make sure the horse is accepting the bit (see page 0).

Too much impulsion sometimes causes crookedness because the horse cannot cope with himself if he is going too fast.

The horse may not be accepting the control of the rider's legs in the approach to the halt. He must allow the rider to 'hold' the quarters.

The rider should also be able to control the shoulders of the horse and not allow the horse to put more weight onto one shoulder than the other.

If the halt is crooked, the rider should not attempt to correct it by using one leg and then the other, this will only cause more crookedness. He may try to go forward a couple of strides to straighten the horse, or he may try to move the forehand a little to get it in line with the quarters, but this is more difficult, and the horse and rider need to understand the shoulder-in exercise (see page 66).

Croup high

This can be seen most easily in canter and piaffe and means that the croup of the horse is going up at each stride which is incorrect. The hindquarters should lower and the hind legs come under the horse more and more during training in order to lighten the forehand.

CORRECTION
Once established it is difficult to correct, and is usually caused by stiffness and/or being on the forehand. If the balance is correct and the horse is accepting the bit with a round back, the rider should aim to increase the activity of the hind legs, progressively encouraging them to come under the body by using gait variation. (For comments on balance, see page 15.)

When the hind legs are better engaged and come under the body, the croup will have to lower so that the horse's weight is carried by the hindquarters, not the forehand.

Cutting corners

This refers to the degree that the rider takes, or does not take, when riding his horse into the corners of the arena. There is much confusion over this; some riders go straight into the corner and turn sharply to get out, and some waste a lot of the arena by not going anywhere near the corner.

CORRECTION
With this problem, riders must bear in mind the stage of training of their horse. Obviously the more supple and trained the horse the deeper the rider can go into the corner. In the early stages when the horse is not yet collected, it is a

mistake to go too deep and risk upsetting the gait and balance of the horse.

A rough guide to the riding of a corner is as follows. Take two points on either side of the corner and ride a true curve between them with the horse bent in the direction he is going. A wrong bend in the corners or no bend at all is incorrect. (See Fig. 5.)

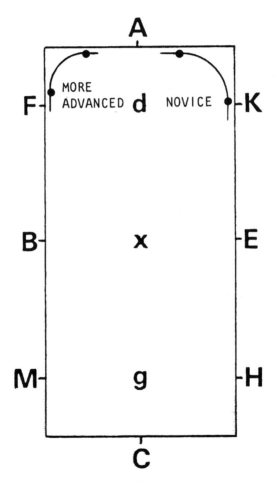

Fig. 5 Riding corners correctly

Disobedient

This remark is frequently used by judges when the horse is evading the rider's aids and not performing the movement required.

CORRECTION

Because obedience is required, the horse must be taught to answer the aids when given.

Some riders find it difficult to be firm enough with their own 'pet' horse, but it is to the horse's own advantage to know exactly what he is meant to be doing; it is much the same as teaching a child to behave. It is sometimes necessary to be cruel to be kind!

Riders must try to be consistent with their aids. It must be very muddling for the horse if the aids vary from one moment to another.

The acceptance of the bit (see page 0) has been talked about earlier.

The horse may be taught to obey the legs with the help of the schooling whip. There is no reason why the horse should be frightened if the whip is correctly introduced, but he should have a very healthy respect for it and jump to attention when it is applied. The rider should be able to 'tap' him with it to increase activity, not beat him to extract forward momentum! When learning, the horse may have to be hit sufficiently hard several times before he will give the rider what he wants but by this action and the *subsequent reward* he will learn.

What do I mean by subsequent reward? All that is necessary to teach the horse that he has complied correctly to the aids is a pat on the neck. Titbits are a nuisance. The horse cannot be stopped five times round the school for a lump of sugar, but he can have five pats on the neck and does learn very quickly from it.

Disunited

This comment refers to the horse in canter when the sequence of the legs becomes, or is, incorrect. For left canter the correct sequence is:

Off hind
Near hind and off fore
Near fore.

When the canter is disunited the sequence could be:

Off hind
Near hind and near fore
Off fore

or

Near hind
Off hind and off fore
Near fore

Quite often the horse will change legs behind (i.e. change the hind leg sequence) on a circle or corner. Sometimes he will change in front only. The situation is generally caused by lack of balance, and/or stiffness in the back.

CORRECTION
The first thing to do is to ensure that the horse is working in balance, and that he is also accepting the bit (see page 9) because resistance in the mouth will hinder any corrections.

The next important factor is the control of the hind-quarters. The horse must be taught to 'listen' to the rider's outside leg which should control any outward swing of the quarters. If the hind legs do not follow the forelegs it will be easy for the horse to change behind, particularly on a circle when he is asked for bend. The rider must be careful when asking for flexion to the inside that he is not using more rein then leg, and that he is controlling the outside of the horse as much as the inside. He must maintain an even pressure on both sides of the horse whenever possible. (For comments on balance, see page 15.)

Did not change diagonal

Some judges do make this comment about the rider, although marks are not deducted. They mean that in the trot, when a change of rein is made the rider has not changed from one diagonal to the other. The horse trots in two-time, first, one foreleg and the opposite hind leg come to the ground, then the other foreleg and the opposite hind leg. These are called diagonals and in rising trot the rider will rise on one pair of legs and sit when the other pair come to the ground.

CORRECTION
A rider correction. He must learn how to change from one diagonal to the other and to feel which one he is on without looking to see. It is necessary to do this when changing the rein in order to show that the horse's muscles are evenly developed on both sides. There are very many horses who are very uneven and subsequently very stiff on one side because of being ridden on one diagonal only.

When first learning to judge the diagonal the rider may glance at the outside foreleg or shoulder. When that foreleg comes to the ground and the shoulder comes back, the rider should sit. To change the diagonal the rider must sit for one extra stride and then continue rising.

Down in front

This is really just another way of saying 'on the forehand', except that on the forehand relates to the weight of the horse on the shoulders whereas 'down in front' implies that the whole front of the horse is too low, not just the shoulders.

CORRECTION
The rider must work on the balance primarily, and by the use of half halts (see page 12) transfer weight from the forehand to the quarters.

He should also consider the outline or silhouette of the horse, and if the neck and head are below the withers, this must surely mean that the front is too low.

By correcting the balance, the outline should improve, but if it does not improve sufficiently, the rider should seek practical expert help.

Dragging hind feet

This describes the horse in rein-back when instead of picking up the hind feet to achieve the steps the horse simply drags each one back making a furrow in the ground.

CORRECTION
The cause of this problem is stiffness of the joints of the hind legs or of the horse's back, or resistance to the aids. The horse may become hollow or simply rigid. Improvement should take place if the horse is made to be rounder in his outline, better acceptance of the bit is acquired and better engagement maintained. If the hind legs of the horse tend to be inflexible, work on improving activity in walk and trot and use of transitions should help.

Dropping impulsion

This means that the horse started with sufficient impulsion but as he went through the movement it became reduced.

CORRECTION

Maintaining impulsion is one of the rider's chief concerns in order to produce work of quality. Any easing off in the rider's concentration or effort may allow the horse time to reduce his own effort, which can result in loss of impulsion.

Regaining it during a test can be difficult, so much of the training is aimed at eliminating this possibility by consistent riding and use of the aids.

Dwelling

This term is used when there is too much lift (elevation) in trot, but insufficient impulsion to take the horse forward.

CORRECTION

Some horses have a lot of natural suspension between each pair of diagonal legs and, to avoid making an effort in trot, can develop a habit of producing a moment of hesitation which is a means of evading going forward properly. This results in a passage type of trot which is incorrect. Such horses may have to be ridden out of their natural tempo for a short time until they will go forwards on command and more willingly to the leg. Suppling exercises and improvement in submission will assist in removing this problem.

Early to walk/trot etc.

A requirement in the tests is to perform the transitions at various markers. This shows the obedience, suppleness and willingness of the horse to comply with his rider's wishes. In some cases the horse may anticipate or simply change the gait before he is told.

CORRECTION

The rider should practise transitions at a marker. When the rider's leg is level with the marker the horse should be doing that which he has been asked. This shows good preparation by the rider.

A young horse needs plenty of warning about a coming transition.

The rider should use half halts to help the horse adjust his balance in order to make the transition smooth, straight and at the designated place. (For comments on half halts, see page 12.)

Earthbound

This generally applies to the canter or the piaffe. If relating to the canter it means that there is no clear moment of suspension. If the term is used for piaffe it means that impulsion has been lost and the horse shuffles from one foot to the other instead of showing clear diagonal steps.

CORRECTION
To correct the canter the rider should concentrate on making the horse go forward more in a rounder outline and obtaining better engagement and impulsion.

In piaffe the same applies, and, in addition, better response to the aids is needed. Many horses fail in piaffe in the arena because their riders have relied too much on their trainer's assistance from the ground, instead of ensuring that the horse understands the exercise properly and responds to the aids.

Falling in

This applies to the horse when, at any gait, he goes round a corner or circle leaning over to the inside, or putting too much weight on the inside shoulder. He might do it momentarily, or most of the time.

CORRECTION
Riders must be aware that the horse needs to be upright when cornering or circling, i.e. the horse's shoulders are taking even weight and that the inside shoulder is not overloaded. To do this, the bend and the response to the rider's inside leg should be improved.

If the horse 'lies' on the rider's leg and ignores his aid to create bend or push him out to the circle the rider should use the schooling whip to make the horse 'listen' to the leg, and make sure he is yielding properly to the bit on the inside.

It is probably best to work at walk and achieve a better bend at that gait. Then work up to the other gaits. The horse often uses too much impulsion causing him to lean against his rider's leg, so probably he will need slowing down and the impulsion temporarily reduced.

Falling onto inside shoulder

Lack of correct bend is the usual cause of this problem because it allows the horse to take more weight onto his inside shoulder instead of distributing it equally.

CORRECTION
In all exercises the balance of the horse is the rider's main responsibility because without it the quality of the work is diminished. Balance is achieved by endeavouring to divide the load between the horse's four legs and, in time, to transfer weight from the heavier part (the forehand) to the hindquarters which, by greater engagement, allow the hind legs to come under the horse's body to carry him.

A horse does not operate satisfactorily by leaning over on corners and circles like a bicycle but needs to be upright. To achieve this the rider must maintain a balanced position himself and use his aids effectively, especially the inside leg, to help the horse.

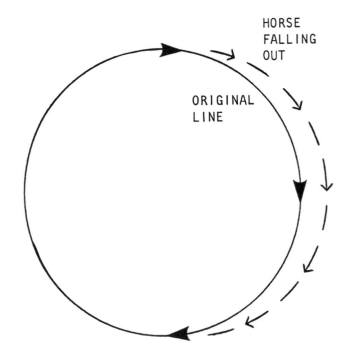

Fig. 6 Horse falling out

Falling out

This may mean that the horse's outside shoulder is escaping on a corner, circle, or in shoulder-in, etc., or it may mean that the whole horse is leaving the original line to the outside. (See Fig. 6.)

If the comment was, 'quarters falling out' it would mean that the forehand was in the correct position, but the quarters had left the original line.

CORRECTION
Many riders are not sufficiently aware that the outside of the horse needs just as much, or more, control as the inside. Because so much is talked about 'bend', they concentrate their efforts on the inside rein. However, this frequently

causes much more bend in the neck than in the rest of the horse; this is incorrect and not a true bend.

If the rider thinks more about the outside rein, both for control and support, he should avoid losing the outside shoulder. If he also makes quite certain he does not have too much bend in the neck this should help too.

If the whole horse 'falls out' when bend is created, then the rider's outside leg and rein are both at fault.

Fell into trot

This describes what sometimes happens to the horse in the transition from the canter to the trot.

As the aid to slow up is given, because the horse's balance in canter is lacking the weight rushes forward and the whole forehand is overloaded at the point when the transition is made.

CORRECTION
The canter should be improved. Many riders do not spend sufficient time in making their canters rhythmic and balanced.

The canter should not be only one speed, it should be adjustable. The rider should be able to shorten and lengthen the stride without resistance to the hand and leg.

Some improvement can be made to the canter by work on a 20 m diameter circle.

First get the horse into his normal canter with the correct bend. Then try to gain more control by using half halts (see page 12). When a slower and/or shorter step is achieved the rider should try to hold these steps for a short distance then go forward again.

With the short steps, the tension on the rein must not be the same the whole time. The rider must always feel and then ease to make certain that he is not 'carrying' the horse, who must be able to maintain his balance and carry himself with a light rein contact.

When the canter can be shortened with the horse in balance, the rider may then try to work on the transition into trot. The trot aid should be given, and when the horse 'breaks' the rider must control the trot strides immediately and also try to balance them, not allowing the horse to race forward.

The horse's back should be rounded in the transition so his head must not on any account be pulled up, but neither should he be allowed to 'dive' down.

It may help the rider to rise in the first few strides of trot, until it is controlled because this will prevent any inadvertant bumping about which the rider may do if the transition is a little rough at first.

When the horse is balanced in the transition, the rider may wish to sit so as to be able to engage the hindquarters properly for the trot.

Flat canter

This remark is usually used when there is insufficient suspension between the canter strides.

CORRECTION
Each three-time stride in the canter should be followed by a moment of suspension when the horse is in the air.

Stiffness in the back and the hind legs not sufficiently under the horse often cause a flat canter. Improvement can be made by first controlling the speed, this will automatically help the hind legs to come under the horse, help him to 'carry' himself and, instead of merely thrusting him forward, will start to push him up a little as well. Thus the canter begins to have a 'jump' in it and the suspension will improve. The rider should then concentrate on the rhythm and regularity.

If there is stiffness in the back, the rider should employ the shoulder-in exercise (see page 66) to improve the horse's suppleness.

Forging

This is when the toe of the hind shoe catches on the heel of the foreshoe and makes a clicking noise. It happens mainly in trot, and might occur occasionally or quite a lot.

CORRECTION
The problem is almost entirely due to lack of balance, so this is where to start the improvement.

Sometimes a horse will begin to forge if he is overtired, so this should be borne in mind. (For comments on balance, see page 15.)

Four-time

This comment describes the canter when the footfalls are all separate instead of in a sequence of three-time.

The correct sequence should be:

Outside hind leg
Inside hind leg, outside foreleg together
Inside foreleg

CORRECTION
This situation almost always occurs owing to lack of impulsion, so this is the first thing to try to correct.

Horses which have flat or broken canters, may also canter in four-time. (For comments on impulsion, see page 43.)

Grinding teeth

This is a most annoying habit and one which loses a mark per movement if it occurs.

Instead of a true acceptance of the bit and hands, the horse will grind his teeth together for various reasons, such as being upset, excited or merely resistant.

CORRECTION

Make certain that the horse is not apprehensive or tense and that he fully understands the aids.

If the horse is relaxed in his body, then the rider should concentrate very patiently on improving the understanding and acceptance of the aids, using plenty of repetition and reward to improve the horse's confidence in his rider.

If the grinding becomes too much of a habit it is almost impossible in some cases to make a correction, so the rider should really go back in his work and start again, concentrating on the horse's state of mind.

Overexcitement is often the cause of the horse starting to grind, or it is a demonstration of impatience. In this case the rider should keep the impulsion subdued and try to calm the horse.

Head up

A momentary evasion of the horse, coming above the bit. Often horses put their heads up for a moment when moving into canter.

CORRECTION

The rider must, from the beginning, work to obtain the acceptance of the bit. He must work the horse in a co-ordinated way keeping enough impulsion so that the horse can go forward without struggling, but not too much which might cause him to lose his balance. If the balance is correct, the head position should be steady and there should be no alteration.

The rider must maintain the steadiness of the position by the co-ordination of his leg and hand, and the steadiness of his contact. If the contact is loose or intermittent the horse's head is unlikely to be still. (For comments on acceptance of the bit, see page 9.)

Hollow back

Means that the top line of the horse from the nose to the tail is concave as opposed to convex.

CORRECTION
A hollow back is incorrect because the horse's head and hindquarters are in such a position that he cannot perform in balance, come on the bit, or engage the hindquarters. It is, therefore, a disaster!

First correct the mouth, bringing the horse's head to a position where the bit can act properly. If the mouth is put right, everything else should improve.

The horse should be worked at a slow speed in order to bring the hind legs underneath him, and the rider should temporarily avoid sitting trot until the horse is able to use his back instead of holding it stiffly away from the rider. In some cases it may be necessary to work the horse with his head very low, in order to stretch the back muscles, but this does not mean that he should be allowed to go on the forehand.

He should be worked in balance, and only then should the rider allow, or encourage, the head to lower for a few strides or maybe a few minutes. The horse having had the chance to round his back and stretch and relax the muscles, should then be asked to come up into the correct position and work on. The rider may wish to read further about acceptance of the bit and balance, (see pages 9 and 15).

Hurried

This term usually refers to the gaits and means that the horse is rushing along without showing any real rhythm.

It can also mean that a turn such as a pirouette has been hurried, lacking rhythm and control.

CORRECTION

First, slow down, even if it feels as though you have no impulsion, then, really think about creating some regular rhythm in the stride at the various gaits.

It may help to count the footfalls, the walk four-time, trot two-time and canter three-time, but riders should try to develop a feel for rhythm coming from an awareness of balance and length of stride.

Halt early or late

This means that the horse has halted before or after the marker.

CORRECTION

There may be various reasons why a halt comes in the wrong place such as resistance to the aids, lack of impulsion etc., but generally it is up to the rider to make it accurate. He should aim to halt when his leg is level with the marker and in the case of halt at 'A', when the horse's body is directly over the centre line. Marks are often lost because this is not complied with.

Immobility insufficient

This comment applies to a halt that is not completely immobile. The horse may have altered his head position, or moved a leg, or merely not halted long enough. Sometimes a test will state the length of time for a halt.

CORRECTION

Every well-mannered horse should halt and stand still and it is one of the first things for the rider to insist upon.

Some horses, especially thoroughbreds, get rather fidgety, and some even threaten to rear, if made to stand. If the horse gets worked up over halts, the rider must try to calm him and get him more relaxed.

Avoid holding on to the reins too tightly at the halt. Make sure the horse is only on a light contact with the hand and leg.

Once he is relaxed, practise plenty of halts from walk and pat him when he does stand still. Try to keep him straight because if he stops in balance he will be more likely to keep still.

Impulsion lacking

The remark is made if the horse has insufficient energy to keep him going forward at a regular speed, or if he is almost dropping into a lower gait.

CORRECTION
There is a general misunderstanding about impulsion. It is not speed. It is the energy in the hindquarters, which can be built up by the use of exercises, so that the horse is able to propel himself forward without difficulty, and do what his rider wishes. If the hind legs are not underneath the horse's body, the impulsion will be misplaced and if they are working behind the quarters, the horse will be thrusting forward all the time and will not be balanced.

If the hind legs are well under the horse he can push himself up a little as well as forward, which will give spring to the stride and the ability to support himself, his weight and that of his rider.

In the early stages of a horse's training too much impulsion should not be expected. If the rider creates a lot of energy in the quarters, the horse will not have the balance to cope with it. Therefore the impulsion must be sufficient for the horse to work actively in balance, and only gradually, as training progresses and the horse develops his physique, may the impulsion be built up.

When horses lack impulsion, it is generally because they have been brought to a slower speed without the rider making sure that the hind legs remain active.

The schooling whip may be employed to make the hindquarters work more, i.e. the flexion of all the joints, rather than making the horse go faster. A longer stride is not necessarily required.

Inactive

This remark applies when the hind legs of the horse are not coming under him and the hocks are not bending but remaining rather straight.

CORRECTION
An active hind leg is one which bends at the hock and comes well under the horse's body, so that he can push himself up a little and forward, with maximum effect and minimum effort.

To make a lazy horse active, the rider must use the aid of the schooling whip. Because of its length it can be used lightly on the quarters, without the rider removing his hand from the reins and thus disturbing the contact.

The rider must not drive the horse forward at a fast speed. In fact, the hocks are usually made more active at a fairly slow speed, because they have to work a lot harder.

The whip may have to be used quite a lot to begin with until the lazy horse learns to respect the leg and respond to it when it is applied lightly.

A few taps of the whip on a reasonably well-schooled horse will increase the energy in the hindquarters and make the hind legs more active.

Inattentive

The horse is not listening to the aids of his rider; his mind is elsewhere and his attention is outside the arena.

CORRECTION

From the beginning of his training the young horse should pay attention to what he is being asked to do and learn to obey the aids. Young horses must learn to concentrate on what they are being taught and not on what is going on around them.

Some are better at this than others, so it is a good idea to work a horse in places where there are distractions. Start with one thing at a time, things like other animals, the dog, the cat, cows, sheep etc., then traffic. Cars which rush past on the other side of the hedge can be most distracting. Horses will be distracted by almost anything: birds, flapping plastic flags, paper bags, umbrellas, even leaves falling in the hedge!

Although the young horse will be startled to begin with he will gradually accept all these things and will learn to ignore them providing his rider is firm and does not let him look around and as long as his aids keep the horse's attention. Some horses are genuinely frightened by distractions and need to be calmed whereas others are just naughty.

Insufficient impulsion.

See *Impulsion lacking*, page 43.

Interrupted

This remark refers to the piaffe steps when they have started in rhythm, have altered in tempo, height or quality and have then returned to the original rhythm.

CORRECTION

All control over rhythm, tempo and regularity depends upon the straightness of the horse, his balance, suppleness and submission. In piaffe the horse may drop 'behind the leg' so focus should be put on engagement and forward inclination together with roundness.

Irregular

This refers to the stride of the horse when one or more strides are in a different rhythm, or are shorter or longer than the others.

CORRECTION
If the horse is worked at home consistently, in a regular rhythm, and the rider controls the length of the strides, he will learn to carry himself correctly and stay regular at each gait.

Occasionally there may be an alteration due to a piece of uneven ground, a momentary loss of balance, or a mistake made by the rider such as an involuntary shift of weight, movement of leg, hand etc. This is unfortunate but not a serious mistake, as long as the horse is working normally with good regularity.

If the horse repeatedly gets this comment in a test, the rider must take a serious view of this fault because consistent irregularity will lose many marks.

The steps may be irregular owing to the mouth not being quite even on both sides or there being an evasion of the bit. Or, the horse may be more stiff on one side than the other and may not be taking equal length steps. This will mean suppling exercises such as shoulder-in to make the muscle development even, and more concentration by the rider to control the steps. (For additional comments on acceptance of the bit and shoulder-in, see pages 9 and 66.)

Jumped into canter

Sometimes in transition from trot to canter the horse will literally make a stride as though about to jump something, with the front legs higher off the ground than the hind legs. The head usually goes up too and the neck is raised.

CORRECTION
The horse must be made more obedient to the rider's aid, giving an immediate but smooth reaction to a light aid. Practise going from canter to trot to canter on a circle, demanding an instant answer to each aid. The horse will then become more alert and will be waiting for some directive instead of plodding round mentally asleep. If he should raise his head, neck and forehand, he is not going forward with enough impulsion, the canter-trot-canter exercise should improve this also.

Laboured

This describes a gait or a movement when it is a tremendous effort for the horse and he can hardly cope with it.

CORRECTION
Improve the activity and impulsion by using the schooling whip and riding transitions to get the hindquarters under the horse. If he is better balanced and more active he will be able to do what is asked more easily. (For additional comments on balance and impulsion, see page 15 and 43.)

Lacking bend

This could refer to bend in lateral work, or more simply, bend in corners or on circles etc.

CORRECTION
Whenever there is a curve in the arena or in a movement, the horse should show a curve equivalent to that of the exercise, i.e. on a 10 m circle the bend will be greater than on a 20 m circle. The horse should be uniformly curved from nose to tail. He should be bent round the rider's inside leg in the direction in which he is going. If there is a lack of

bend, it will be due to ineffective use of the aids, particularly the rider's inside leg.

Lacking collection

Means that when collection is asked for, the amount shown by horse and rider is insufficient.

CORRECTION
It may be difficult to gauge the amount of collection required because so many different examples of it are seen. Some riders go quite slowly with a lot of elevation. Some ride much more forward.

Some requirements are obvious. The horse must show that he can come together more. His quarters must be lowered slightly and his hind legs come well under him. He must be very active and full of controlled energy. The forehand must be light, with the head and neck raised, the head bent at the poll and lower jaw relaxed showing no resistance. The horse is compressed into a ball of lightly controlled impulsion.

If any of the above aspects are not seen, the collection may be insufficient.

To achieve true collection requires a tremendous amount of dedicated work on the basic schooling, i.e. straightness, balance, acceptance of the bit, etc. If any of these are lacking the collection will never be really good.

Lacking expression

Judges will sometimes say this about flying changes when the stride is short, dull or mechanical. This does not mean that the change of leg is incorrect, simply lacking flair and life.

CORRECTION
The brief answer to this is to ride the flying changes forward more and enjoy them! Of course, when anxious not to make a mistake, riders are content with moderate impulsion. Because part of the art of dressage is to combine the horse's natural joie de vivre with accuracy and obedience, riders must beware of erring on the side of safety with correct sequences which are perhaps on the forehand and lacking engagement, and try for changes which are still correct but bolder and livelier.

Lacking impulsion.

See *Impulsion lacking,* page 43.

Lacking purpose

This term is used to describe extended walk when it is rather dreary and takes horse and rider an age to get across the arena!

CORRECTION
There are many bad walks to be seen in dressage competitions; some horses have a naturally bad walk with little or no extension, and some are man-made. More often than not, a walk can be improved if the rider keeps the horse on the aids, and does not allow him to slop along or drop the engagement. Some riders are intimidated by a tense horse who may jog if the leg is kept on, but this is obviously a flaw in their training. If the rider teaches the horse correct acceptance of the hand and leg, then he will be able to ride forewards boldy.

Lacking rhythm

A gait or movement which lacks rhythm is one which does not have regular even steps.

CORRECTION

A good deal of concentration is required by the rider.

Some horses naturally have a good rhythm and some do not. Even horses who do not can be corrected if ridden carefully. The rider must aim at a steady controlled speed, without too much impulsion to start with, and regular steps with even length.

It may help to count the footfalls in the various gaits.

If the horse is not relaxed mentally and physically he will not develop his rhythm, so any tenseness or stiffness must be avoided or overcome. (For comments on footfalls, see pages 20, 30, 39, 42 and 81.)

Late behind

This is a comment made with reference to the flying change. In the moment of suspension at canter the horse should make the flying change.

In a true change the fore and hind leg on the same side come forward together, but when late behind, the foreleg may come first followed by the hind leg a stride or half stride later. Some judges may use the expression 'late change' to mean the same thing but 'late change' can also mean late to the rider's aid!

CORRECTION

If the horse persistently changes late behind, it can be very difficult to put right, and it is probably best to put the problem into the hands of an expert. If the rider wishes to attempt the correction himself he should first make sure that the canter itself is good and the horse is not hollowing his back. The strides must be big and round with a clear moment of suspension.

Work on the simple changes through walk and trot. The horse should be able to change from one leg to the other with only one stride at walk or trot between the canters and must be extremely obedient to the aids. The rider, when he asks for the flying change, must ask a fraction before the moment of suspension so that the horse, after the period in the air, lands on the new leading leg.

Late to aid

This remark refers to the flying changes, when the rider has obviously given an aid but the horse's response is delayed. This is most relevant when the change is asked for at a specific marker. If the change does not occur it is obviously an inaccuracy.

CORRECTION
From the start of training the horse should learn to answer an aid when it is given and should receive a reprimand when he does not, or praise when he does. Sometimes, however, owing to slow thinking, or perhaps insufficient preparation by the rider, a response to a request may be delayed. Clear consistant aids should overcome the problem, with, if necessary, a little encouragement from the schooling whip. Some riders fail to use sufficient inside leg to send the horse forward in flying changes so attention should be given to this.

Late to start

This means, literally, that a movement which should have begun at a certain marker has not done so.

CORRECTION
This fault can occur for two main reasons. Firstly, the horse has failed to respond to the aids, or, secondly, the rider has mistakenly or sometimes deliberately not given them.

If the horse has not been asked to respond for some reason best known to the rider, he can only expect to be penalised for inaccuracy. If the horse fails to respond, then presumably the preparation was not satisfactory or the aids given were inadequate.

Leaning in.

See *Falling in,* Page 34.

Leaning on the bit

The horse is relying on the hands of his rider for support. There is too much weight on the forehand and in particular on the bit.

CORRECTION
Using half halts, the rider must improve the balance to reduce the weight on the forehand. He must then teach the horse to accept the bit so that he will rest on it lightly.

There is nothing more exhausting for the rider than a horse leaning on the bit and it is quite unnecessary to put up with it as many riders seem to do. It does require rather a lot of hard work but it is worth the effort. (For additional comments on the acceptance of the bit, half halts and balance, see pages 9, 12 and 15.)

Lengthening insufficient

This could apply to any increase in the length of stride within a gait, i.e. collected to working, working to extended etc., where the horse does not show enough difference between the two.

CORRECTION
Most horses find it almost impossible to lengthen correctly before they can shorten the stride. Therefore I think it is necessary to teach the horse to carry himself on a short stride in order to put the hindquarters in a position where they can propel him forward without difficulty.

Once the hind legs are under the horse he can be asked to 'push off' and give some length. The degree of length must necessarily depend on the stage of the horse's training. It is a great mistake to make the horse stretch too far before he is ready because it may cause him to place his hind legs behind him which impedes true impulsion and is much more of a strain on the loins.

When showing a longer stride the rider must know what is required for the standard at which he is riding and make sure that he defines the transitions before and after the lengthening.

Loop on two tracks

Some of the movements in the tests require the horse – when cantering – to either return to the track after a half circle on the same leg, or make a loop up the side of the arena which involves a small amount of counter canter. Sometimes on the return to the track, instead of the hind legs following the forelegs, the horse will go sideways in half pass. This defeats the object of the exercise and so will be marked down. (See Figs. 7–10.)

CORRECTION
Try to make sure that the hind legs are following the forelegs, and that the hindquarters are under control.

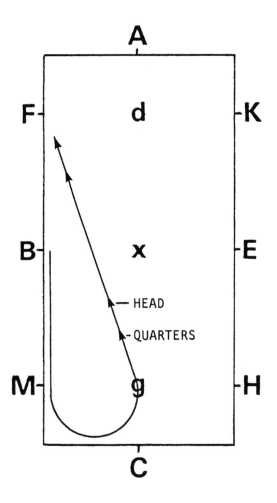

Fig. 7 Correct

54

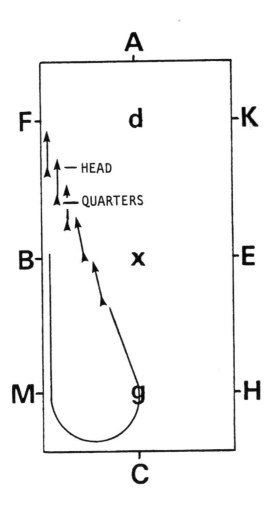

Fig. 8 Incorrect

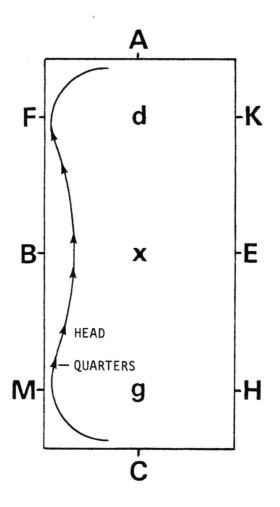

Fig. 9 Correct

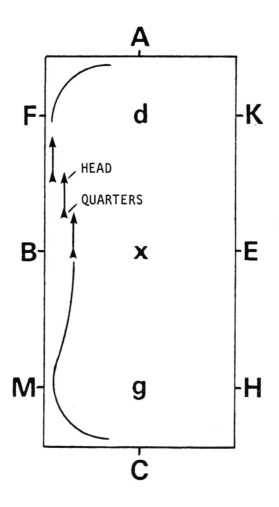

Fig. 10 Incorrect

57

Loops not equal

There are various movements involving three or more loops. They should be of equal size and if they are not, marks are lost.

CORRECTION
The rider is obviously responsible for the size and equality of the loops. Often they are not ridden equally because the horse is easier on one rein than the other. The very reason for the exercise is to prove that the horse can perform well on both reins and that his muscles are evenly developed. Most horses do find work easier on one side just as people are right- or left-handed.

Riders should be aware that they themselves are stronger on one side and weaker on the the other and must be careful when schooling not to have the wrong effect on their horses.

An equal amount of work on both reins is important but if the horse is finding the work difficult on one rein, work him a little more on that side until it becomes easier.

Lost bend

This would mean quite simply that although the bend has been correct, it is altered for a moment, or longer, becoming straight or incorrect (outward as opposed to inward).

CORRECTION
Maintaining a bend means that the rider has to be constantly aware of the bend he wants, and keeps it with consistant aids. Bends are frequently lost owing to insufficient use of the inside leg of the rider because, without this initially, all other aids become ineffective.

Lost rhythm

This applies to a rhythmic stride which, for one reason or another, loses the rhythm briefly.

CORRECTION
If there is already a rhythm in the gaits, a momentary loss is not all that serious, unless it recurs frequently.

The rider should check on his balance and try to ride with more concentration. (For comments on balance, see page 15).

Moved at halt

This comment refers to when the horse has made the halt satisfactorily and then made a movement of the head, or perhaps stepped back, rested a leg, or shifted the quarters slightly.

CORRECTION
The rider must make sure that he can halt and stand still at any given moment and in a variety of circumstances, such as wind, rain, etc.

The horse must know that to move is not allowed and that he will be scolded, but when he stands still he may be given a pat or word of praise.

Muddled steps

This comment may be made to describe rein-back steps which are of uneven height or length or are inaccurate in number. (See also *No clear steps*.)

CORRECTION
Riders should try to be distinct about the start and finish to the rein-back because one half-step at either end could spoil

the whole movement. This happens when the horse shows reluctance to start owing to some resistance or is behind the rider's leg during the first steps and then carries on by himself after the rider has given the forward aid. Any half-step or resistance by the horse could cause problems, making the exercise look a muddle.

Neck too short

This is a rather ambiguous term because it sounds as though the judge is criticising the conformation of the horse. This is not the intention. It means that the rider has drawn in the front of the horse by hand aids which are too strong and not brought the hindquarters up under the horse in the correct manner, before taking hold of the front.

CORRECTION
Throughout the horse's training the rider must consider the horse's mouth and the engagement of the hindquarters. There must be no resistance in the mouth because this prevents the hindquarters from becoming engaged. On the other hand the horse must be going forward in order to 'make the mouth'.

The two must, therefore, develop together. By equal use of the hand and leg the rider must bring the horse together. Pressure by the hands that is not supported by the legs can give the appearance of the forehand or neck being shortened, therefore the rider must work hard to equalize the pressure of hand on the rein and leg on the horse's sides.

Obviously, for a moment, one may be heavier than the other but always aim at returning to equal pressure.

No clear steps

This term would apply to the rein-back or the piaffe. In rein-back it would denote that the steps were muddled (see also

Muddled steps), some shorter, some longer, some in two-time and some one step at a time. This would obviously make the exercise look a mess, and it would be impossible to be accurate with the required number of steps.

In piaffe it would mean that diagonal steps were not achieved.

CORRECTION

To correct the problem in rein-back, a good halt must be obtained first with the horse really on the aids to ensure that when he is asked to go back he is in the best possible position to comply. During the rein-back the poll should be the highest point of the forehand, and steps are often spoilt because it is not. Rushing backwards, reluctance or steps which are too large should not be allowed because these faults all affect the clearness of the steps. A good rein-back is the result of good submission.

The piaffe will only be successful if there is good engagement of the hindquarters, straightness, well-maintained impulsion, suppleness, roundness and submission so that the horse can spring evenly from one diagonal to the other.

No immobility

This comment could be made whenever there is a halt requiring immobility, and also prior to rein-back when the horse anticipates the request.

CORRECTION

If the rider is aware of the necessity for always keeping the horse strictly on the aids when halting, the horse should expect this control so will not anticipate or be able to anticipate. However if he does try he should be made to wait, and kept in halt until he will stand still. Some horses become very anxious in halt, so use tact to retain calmness.

No lengthening of the frame

In order to cover ground in extensions the horse should be encouraged to stretch his neck slightly and bring his nose just in front of the vertical. If this comment is made, the rider has either prevented this happening or the horse may not have responded to the given aids.

CORRECTION
The rider should first ensure that the horse is sufficiently engaged, has enough impulsion, and that he is round and accepting the bit so that when the aids are given for the extension, providing the horse responds correctly, the rider will be able to allow the horse to reach for the stride. It is common for riders to use the reins for balance in extensions which prevents freedom. Try to avoid this by developing a more secure position in the saddle.

Not accepting hand

This means that there is resistance in the mouth of the horse when contact or extra contact is taken by the hand. It manifests itself in many ways, some of which are opening the mouth, tongue hanging out, coming above the bit, leaning on the bit, tossing the head, etc.

CORRECTION
The correction must be in the acceptance of the bit, discussed on page 9.

However, if the rider expects the horse to accept his hand aids, he must give the horse a contact which is flexible and this needs a good deal of understanding. A contact which never varies is not acceptable because it is a dead feel with no 'conversation' for the horse to follow.

No contact is not acceptable either because the horse then has no security, nor can he answer a light aid because the rein contact has to be taken up by the rider and usually results in a jerk in the mouth.

The rider must aim to start with a firm but gentle contact with no slack in the rein, the variation coming from a slight closing or easing of the fingers which is so slight it would not be seen by an onlooker. Much of the lightness of the hands is achieved by the rider having supple elbows and wrists, and good concentration.

Not always true sequence

Judges mainly use this term to describe a walk which has come out of the correct four-beat sequence of steps.

CORRECTION
Losing the correct sequence is often caused by trying to collect the walk too early on in the training or trying to collect without proper engagement and suppleness. Care should be taken to collect by degrees and only when the horse is sufficiently supple and submissive.

Not a true half pass

Half passes require a bend round the rider's inside leg in the direction in which he is going. Any effort failing in this respect could be deemed to be 'not true'.

CORRECTION
The less experienced rider may find lateral work difficult owing to the high degree of co-ordination necessary, and/or lack of knowledge. It is not uncommon to see horses pushed sideways with little or no bend. A correct half pass can only take place if there is a true bend round the rider's inside leg. The rider and horse should look at the marker to which they are travelling with the horse's shoulders positioned towards the marker. Once the position is effected, concentration can be kept on maintaining engagement and impulsion.

Not between hand and leg

This statement usually means that the horse is not sufficiently under control because the rider's hand and leg aids are not co-ordinated. If the co-ordination is lacking then the horse can escape and instead of being brought together by the rider, his body, left to its own devices, will be inclined to wander.

CORRECTION
Some riders are fortunate to have natural co-ordination and seldom have to think about it. Those who do not, have to work hard. They should aim to have equal pressure leg to hand, i.e. never allow the hands to work more strongly than the legs, and vice-versa. There are obviously going to be moments when there must be some alteration. This advice is only a basis on which to work.

The hands and legs are there to 'talk' to the horse and constantly tell him what to do and where to go. If the contact of both are unsteady the conversation will be disjointed and the understanding not clear.

Therefore good co-ordination is vital to the horse's ability to obey his rider. Riders, please note!

Not covering the ground

This term could be used for an extended canter meaning that the canter stride was faster rather than bigger. In this case the stride would be flat instead of, correctly, showing a good moment of suspension.

CORRECTION
Suspension in canter can only be obtained by having good engagement and impulsion. A horse may have a good canter stride naturally but he will also need to 'make ground' in the moment of suspension. This applies especially in extended canter which must remain in three-beat

sequence not become four-beat as in a gallop. Some horses do not have a good, natural moment of suspension and, although this can be manufactured to an extent with training, it may always be a handicap. All extensions can be improved with good collection which enables the horse to use his hindquarters more powerfully giving the gaits lift and spring.

Not direct

This comment applies to transitions which are not exact, for example, walk to canter and vice versa, halt to trot and piaffe to passage etc. The rider has allowed too gradual a transition through another gait, either because the aids have not been sufficiently effective or because the horse has not responded.

CORRECTION
The aim should be to teach the horse to answer an aid immediately it is given. There should of course be correct preparation and warning by the rider so that the horse is in a position to respond. Non-direct transitions are generally due to lack of sufficient engagement, impulsion and collection.

Not enough angle (shoulder-in)

This comment is usually made in reference to the shoulder-in movement, and means that the rider has not asked the forehand to come sufficiently off the track.

CORRECTION
If the horse has been taught the shoulder-in correctly then it is up to the rider to ask for the correct amount of angle. Sometimes it feels as though you have but the judge disagrees. Therefore, to satisfy the judge, it may be necess-

ary to do a little more than you think is needed.

There are, however, mistakes which we as riders must not make.

It is easy to push the quarters out rather than ride the forehand in off the track. Also, it is easy to get too much bend in the neck only, which is not a true shoulder-in. The rider must remember that it is the whole front of the horse from the saddle forwards which must be positioned, and that the outside rein plays a bigger part than the inside rein in controlling this position.

Another failing is to allow the outside shoulder to fall out, but, again, if the outside rein is used correctly, this should not happen.

When teaching shoulder-in to the young horse, it may help to begin at walk to accustom the horse to the aids. Only when the horse can trot in short steps in preparation for collection can he be asked to shoulder-in at trot, and then only for a short distance.

This is a vital exercise the rider uses all through training to control or position the forehand and it must be done correctly to be of value.

If the rider is doubtful how to begin shoulder-in, here are some suggestions.

Start in walk with a slight flexion to the inside hand to make sure that the horse will yield when the rein is taken. Position the forehand by riding the forelegs off the track after a corner so that the horse is already slightly curved.

When the forelegs are off the track, the hind legs must be kept on the track by the use of the rider's inside leg and the horse asked to maintain impulsion and go sideways by the use of that leg. The rider's outside leg will control the quarters and maintain the bend round the inside leg.

The outside rein will control the direction and the speed plus the positioning. Usually an angle of not more than 45 degrees is acceptable.

The point of the exercise is for the rider to have greater control of the forehand. If he is able to put the forehand where he wants he will be able to position and prepare the horse much better for a variety of movements. He will also be able to effect the straightening of the horse at any time by correcting the front.

Not enough collection

This term is used when the collected gaits are deficient in one way or another, i.e. the hind legs are not engaged enough, the steps are too long, the forehand of the horse is too low.

It can also apply to a particular exercise such as a canter pirouette. The judge not only has to look at the pirouette, but also to see if the horse was sufficiently collected during the movement.

CORRECTION
True collection is one of the most difficult things to achieve and only a master of the art will probably do so. The rest of us must try but these are some common mistakes we must beware of making.
1. One of the most common mistakes is to draw the horse in from the front too much so that his neck is shortened and his nose in but without bringing the body together more or engaging the hind legs.
2. Often the steps are shortened but the impulsion is lost making the horse shuffle.
3. The horse is brought back to a slower speed but the quarters are not asked to be active and the forehand is not raised.

The rider must aim to slow the horse so that he can develop shorter steps and having done so, he must make sure that the hind legs stay active by using the schooling whip, *not* harder leg aids. Do not ask for too much impulsion because the horse must find his own balance in these shorter steps and too much impulsion will create a problem for him.

The rider should only ask for a few steps at a time to start with and although he must 'sit', should not attempt to grind his seat into the saddle. Sit as quietly and as still as possible and let the horse find out how to manage himself.

Half halts should be used to help achieve the shortening.

There must be no resistance to the hand and the horse must stay *straight*.

When the horse has learned to shorten the strides and he is accepting the hand and staying straight, the impulsion may be built up.

Eventually the hindquarters must carry the main load of the horse and the forehand will come higher as the result of their greater ability and strength. All this takes quite a long time and cannot be hurried. The horse must be systematically schooled and his muscles developed by exercises to ensure there is no strain. (For comments on half halts, see page 12.)

Not enough difference

This term is generally used when an alteration within a gait is required, i.e. extension to collection, working to medium, etc. It means that the difference in the length of the stride is not sufficiently shown and the transition from one requirement to the other was not 'marked', and took too long.

CORRECTION
The rider should try to ascertain the difference by watching an expert, or having tuition on the various differences in the gaits, so that he knows what is expected and how much extension or collection he is aiming for.

He must know how to shorten the strides for collection, without restricting the horse, and how to lengthen the strides, without allowing the hind legs to trail behind the horse, or letting him fall on his forehand. He must know how much impulsion is needed and the differences in the outline of the horse.

Generally speaking, in collection, the horse appears more together and comes higher in front having his hind legs further under him, and in extension the neck is slightly stretched giving the appearance of the horse being longer. Having discovered what the differences are, the rider must show by the transitions into and out of the gait variations, the difference between them. For example, if going from a working gait to a medium gait, the rider must show a definite change at the required marker.

When making the change from the medium to the working gait the horse must make the transition at the marker in a very few strides, not drift into it.

Not enough extension

This means that the horse is not showing enough length of stride.

CORRECTION
The rider must bear in mind that the various standard tests require different degrees of extension, e.g. the extension in Elementary dressage tests is not so great as in Medium dressage tests. However, the basic requirements for extension are the same and only the amount asked for varies.

Firstly the horse must be capable of placing his hind legs correctly so that he can carry himself without losing balance and rhythm.

Secondly, he must be able to cope with the necessary impulsion. The rider must not try to ask for the extension before he has achieved a degree of collection.

Only if the horse can collect himself properly will he then be in a position to extend, having the hind legs and the impulsion in the right place.

Many horses who do not show much promise at first, will often show good extension eventually if the collection is improved. (For comments on collection, see page 48.)

Not enough from behind

This term usually means that the hind legs are not doing their job sufficiently and are possibly taking rather a shallow step, not reaching far enough under the horse.

CORRECTION
To develop more 'push' from the hind legs, the rider must first put them in the right place. This means correcting the balance (see page 15), plus making the horse active and building up some impulsion (see page 43).

Once the energy is sufficiently 'stored' in the quarters, the horse should have plenty of power to push himself forward more.

Not finished

This remark may be made with reference to half-pass, when the hindquarters have trailed at the end of the movement instead of finishing behind the forehand before going straight forwards.

CORRECTION
The rider should be conscious of the correct position of the hindquarters in all lateral work. So often they lead or trail especially towards the end of the movement. If the bend of the horse is true, that is to say, correctly bent round the inside leg of the rider, and if the forehand is properly positioned, the aforementioned faults should not occur. However, extra attention should be given to making sure that the movement is finished precisely.

Not forward enough

This may be difficult to understand, but most judges mean

that although the horse may be on the bit and in a nice rhythm etc., he is not working with enough energy and consequently is lacking in stride length and impulsion.

CORRECTION
Without spoiling the balance and rhythm or the head carriage, the rider must ask the horse to be more active (using the schooling whip) and build up a little more impulsion which will help to take the horse forward more.

Make sure that there is no resistance to the hand because this could cause a block, which will prevent the horse from going forward enough. (For additional comments on the acceptance of the bit and impulsion, see pages 9 and 43.)

Not lowering enough

This usually applies to the walk on a long or free rein. When the rider gives the rein, the horse, instead of stretching his neck out and down, does the opposite.

CORRECTION
If the horse does not lower naturally when the rein is eased, the rider should strive to improve the horse's mouth (see page 9) in order to work the neck muscles in such a way that when the rein is given the horse will stretch correctly.

The horse will also probably need suppling exercises such as shoulder-in (see page 66) to stretch the stiff muscles which are holding him back when the rein is given.

Not maintained

There may be a moment during any movement when the movement alters. The comment may refer to an alteration in the regularity of the steps, such as in the passage, or to lateral work where bend or angle are not held, although the latter are normally specified.

CORRECTION

Any change in a gait or in any movement may be due to a loss of balance, impulsion, engagement, resistance, or all four, resulting in quickening or fading of the steps. The rider can prevent this happening by good preparation, a secure seat and sustained effort from his aids.

Not on centre line

This comment is fairly obvious, but it is surprising how often one has to use it when judging and how difficult it seems to be for many horses and riders to remain straight on the centre line.

CORRECTION

Sometimes there is a clearly defined line, sawdust, mown or painted. If so the rider must follow this line and if he has taught his horse to go straight, it should not be a great problem. At home, he must practise on a line making sure that the horse is accustomed to it and will not step aside as he meets it.

If he should wobble off the line, the rider must return to it and not continue on a parallel line next to it because this will lose even more marks.

If there is no defined line, the rider must aim at the 'C' marker, which helps in any case, and keep it in sight between the horse's ears so that he can be held straight.

Not on the aids

This means, basically, that the horse is not sufficiently under the rider's control, i.e. he is escaping from the rider's control, or resisting it. If the comment is applied to only a single movement, it may mean that the situation is temporary, but if it is used as a general comment, the rider is in a serious predicament.

CORRECTION

The aim of all riding, not just dressage, is the effective use of the aids to control the horse. Horses can 'switch off' sometimes, especially temperamental ones, or very idle ones, but the process of riding is request and response, which, if it is to be successful, must be consistant and clear. Riders must have the knowledge to make the requests, the tact and sympathy to transfer them to the horse, plus good 'feel' to recognise when they have been responded to. Only this process will enable the rider to 'talk' to his horse through the aids and obtain willing co-operation.

Not overtracking

In medium, extended and free walk, and medium and extended trot, the imprint of the hind foot of the horse should fall beyond the imprint left by the forefoot on the same side, i.e. the near hind should go beyond the near fore and the off hind beyond the off fore.

CORRECTION

If the horse is not overtracking, he may possibly be restricted, i.e. held back by the rider and not able to take a good length of stride.

The rider must ensure that he allows the horse to move as naturally as possible, particularly in the walk where the stride should be the maximum length that the horse will give. The rider should keep a light contact while allowing the horse to move his head and neck up and down so that he can maintain his balance. Later in the training, the horse will need to be collected in the walk, but many are spoilt by doing this too soon.

In trot, the rider must aim to have the horse relaxed because stiff muscles often cause short strides to occur. With relaxation, good rhythm and balance, the horse should be able to bring his hind legs forward and thus overtrack.

A few horses have a conformation which makes it very difficult or nearly impossible for them to overtrack, but usually some slight improvement can be made.

Not square

This comment refers to the halt and means that the horse has not stopped with a leg at each corner, which he has to if he is to be balanced. The hind feet should be directly behind the forefeet so that, from the front, only the forelegs are seen.

CORRECTION
Some horses will come naturally to a square halt if they are balanced but most horses will stop with one leg not in line with the other, usually a hind leg.

If the horse persistently leaves the same leg back, the rider should use his whip gently on that leg to move it up. Someone should be on the ground to see if the horse halts square or not and to tell the rider which leg is at fault because it is not always easy to tell. The rider should try to concentrate on the movement of the legs in the last strides before the halt. That way he should be able to feel which leg is doing what and, as a result, where they are at the halt. If the rider can develop this feel, the halts should improve.

Also, if there is no resistance in the mouth and the horse is kept up to the bridle with the legs, the halts should come square.

Not straight

This expression occurs many times in many different instances. It may refer to the head and neck, to the body, or the legs.

CORRECTION

From the very first moment the rider sits on his horse, he must aim to achieve perfect straightness to ensure that the horse develops evenly on both sides, takes even steps and does not become one sided. The rider must keep the horse's head and neck directly in front of him to keep the horse straight; many people ride with the front bend round one way all the time. The rider must have an even contact. The horse's body must be kept straight between the rider's legs.

The hind legs must follow the track of the forelegs. The horse must be straight in all his transitions and the transition is not performed unless it is straight. This is one of the very important basic principles to which the rider must pay special attention, because much of the future training depends on this being correct.

Not through

This comment is made when the sequence of legs in a flying change is correct, but the hind leg which is coming forward does not come far enough under the horse's body.

CORRECTION

One cause can be idleness, with the horse reluctant to make enough effort, or another can be 'blocking' in the mouth. 'Blocking' is a resistance to the bit on the same side as the offending hind leg. If the cause is laziness, the horse should be taught to answer the aids better or they should be used to greater effect. If resistance in the mouth is the problem, submission may be improved by use of head flexions to release tension.

Not tracking up

This is when the hind legs of the horse are idle, not reaching the imprint left by the forelegs as they should, except in the collected gaits.

75

CORRECTION

There are two separate problems.

1. You may have a horse which is lazy and lacking impulsion and will not put himself out to take a good length of stride. This horse must be woken up with the use of the schooling whip to encourage him to use more energy to take him forward.

2. The second horse may be the complete opposite, but because he is headstrong, the rider has constantly to restrain him. Instead of taking long strides the horse will take short hurried steps always, seemingly, trying to keep up with himself.

This horse must first be slowed down and made to relax by quiet slow work. Only when relaxed will he then begin to make longer steps but it may take quite a while to obtain the required length. It does take a good deal of patience, and constant correction. The horse should also be allowed to lower his head and neck which will come with the relaxation and will also help to lengthen the strides. Half halts will help with this situation (see page 12).

Off the bit

Maybe the horse has altered his head position for a moment due to loss of balance, resistance to the aids, or the rein contact may be broken by the rider. Sometimes, regrettably, the horse is never on the bit owing to the ignorance of the rider who does not know how to obtain it.

CORRECTION

The rider should first check on the correct acceptance of the bit, and ensure he knows what is right and what the possible evasions are.

Then he should correct the impulsion which may be lacking, thus allowing the horse to drop behind the bridle.

Next the rein contact must be steady and acceptable to the

horse. Then it is up to the rider to concentrate and keep the horse between hand and leg. If his co-ordination is satisfactory the horse should not be able to come off the bit.

A momentary mistake in training is not a major disaster, but continuous mistakes can become a habit and should be avoided. (For acceptance of the bit, see page 9.)

On the forehand

The weight of the horse, instead of being evenly distributed over all four legs, comes forward over the front legs causing the forehand of the horse to be lower than it should be and preventing the horse operating efficiently and easily.

CORRECTION
The answer lies in the balance being improved and the rider being aware that owing to the horse being naturally heavy in front, because of the position of the head and neck, the weight should gradually be transferred back to the hindquarters. The use of half halts and the gradual increase in the strength of the muscles in the hindquarters should be the chief method of transferring the weight.

Once the horse is strong enough and able to put his hind legs sufficiently under the body (the result of systematic work) he should lighten the forehand.

The horse cannot work easily if he is on the forehand. It is a hindrance not only to him, but also to his rider who is constantly pulled forwards with too much weight in his hands; not a comfortable situation and one which is all too common. As well as half halts the rider should try working in better balance and rhythm on circles mainly in trot and use the transitions from trot to walk and vice versa, making sure that the hindquarters are active. (For additional comments on half halts and balance, see pages 12 and 15.)

On the hand

This expression is used when the horse is allowed to lean on the bit using the rider's hands as support.

CORRECTION
Check on the horse's balance because he is probably taking too much weight on the forehand.

Use half halts to correct this. Do not allow the horse to gradually push down on the bit. At all times he must accept the bit. (For additional comments on the acceptance of the bit, half halts and balance, see pages 9, 12 and 15.)

On two tracks

When the horse is going forwards the hind legs should follow the track of the forelegs but sometimes the horse may swing his quarters over, lose his balance or mistake his rider's aids and, instead of going straight forward, there will be some sideways movement as well. Then the horse is said to be on two tracks.

CORRECTION
The rider must be more aware of the importance of the straightness of the horse and of making sure that the hind legs do follow the forelegs, especially on circles and around corners. At no time should the rider's legs allow the quarters to fall in, or fall out.

Check that the head and neck are straight and not bent too much. Very often there is more bend in the neck than in the rest of the horse. Because the inflexibility of the horse's spine only permits the body to make a slight curve, the neck should only curve to the same degree.

A neck with too much bend in it will often make the quarters swing out. The rider then tries to correct this with the outside leg and the horse may swing the other way which will put him on two tracks.

Outline not maintained

Some judges will use the expression 'outline', some 'silhouette', meaning the same thing.

When the outline or silhouette were not maintained, it means that the position of the horse's head and neck, the roundness of his back and the engagement of the quarters were correct at times, but did not stay the same throughout the test.

The outlines are different for the Novice horse compared to the Advanced horse because the centre of balance is further back in the Advanced horse.

CORRECTION
The rider should try to find out from an expert what the correct outline should be for his horse at the various stages of training. Having done so he must endeavour to establish it by working on the acceptance of the bit, the balance and the activity of the hindquarters. When these are under control and steady, the horse will be able to carry himself without disturbance and his outline should stay the same.

Overbent

This expression is used when the horse is bent too much at the poll and the nose is behind the vertical. The horse has the appearance of 'leading' with his forehead.

CORRECTION
The horse becomes overbent for several reasons.
1. He may have too much impulsion and be 'racing' into the bridle. Too much pressure on the bit, caused by the rider trying to gain control, may make him draw his nose in too far, almost onto his chest. The first thing to do is to reduce the impulsion by slowing the horse down to a controllable speed. It will be necessary to use half halts because the pressure on the bit must vary. The rider may

feel that he is going too slowly but this would be preferable to the horse being overstrong. Once a slower speed is established, the rider should endeavour to take a light contact and ride the horse in a normal manner.

2. The horse may also become overbent owing to a lack of impulsion. If the rider is not using his legs adequately, asking the horse to go up into the bridle, the horse may well hang behind the bit with his head overbent at the poll. The rider must maintain the contact with the bit, but increase the activity of the hind legs to create some more impulsion. This should take the horse forward enough to make him raise his head to the correct position.

3. The horse may have been over-bitted or restricted by the rider's hands, but as long as the rider ensures that the bit is acceptable and so are his hands, then these corrections may be applied.

If the horse gets into the habit of being overbent, he may like the idea and however hard the rider tries to make the corrections, the horse may not want to come into the right position. In this case, the rider may have to 'lift' the horse's head and neck by raising one or both hands for a brief moment until it comes into a better position. This may have to be repeated several times to achieve the correction.

A correction will not be achieved by loosening the rein contact. (For comments on half halts, see page 12).

Over the bit

This is similar to being overbent and usually means that the horse is on the forehand, or leaning on the hand, or possibly all three. The weight of the horse is too much on the front and he is not accepting the bit lightly with his head in the correct position.

CORRECTION. See *Overbent*, page 79.

Overtracking.

See *Not overtracking*, page 73.

Pace (gait) not true

This means that the gait which is criticised is not in the correct time, i.e. walk should be four-time, trot two- and canter three-time.

It is possible for the horse to move his legs like a pacer, i.e. both legs on the same side coming forward together. This could occur in walk or trot.

In canter, it is possible for the horse to canter in four-time instead of three-, each hoof coming to the ground at a different time.

There could also be too much suspension in the trot making it more like a passage than trot. This comment might be used in any of these instances.

CORRECTION

The gaits sometimes go wrong because the horse is tense either mentally or physically. Therefore it may be a good idea to make sure that the horse is relaxed and not too keyed up.

Too much or too little impulsion may also cause problems. The rider must, therefore, try to assess whether he is working the horse with the correct amount.

Resistance in the mouth can also cause incorrect gaits, consequently the rider must also check that the horse is accepting the bit.

If the trot is too high and too much like passage, the impulsion must be directed forward more and the tempo of the steps quickened by increasing the speed slightly. (For comments on acceptance of the bit, see page 9.)

Pacing walk

A pacing walk is when the true four-beat sequence of the walk has been lost resulting in the two legs on the same side moving simultaneously, making it look like a march in two-time.

CORRECTION
The problem is usually caused by stiffness through the horse and/or resistance in the back or mouth, therefore more attention to suppleness and correct submission to the aids is needed, plus more careful collection by the rider because tension can also be a cause. There may be difficulty in recognising what is going on, but a pacing walk feels very stilted and swings forwards on one side and then on the other. Pacing can be difficult to cure if it becomes a habit, so particular attention should be given to correct sequence of steps at all times. Slowing the gait generally will help horse and rider because there is then more time to make corrections. Lateral movements can also be used to supple the horse and will often put the horse back into a correct four-time sequence.

Pivoted

This refers to the hind legs of the horse in a pirouette in walk. With a correct pirouette, the hind legs should remain mobile and should march up and down on the spot. If one of the legs 'sticks' and is not picked up, the horse may be said to have pivoted.

CORRECTION
When teaching the horse the pirouette the rider must first be able to collect the walk a little so that the steps are short and bouncy.

The quarters must be well under control and when the turn is commenced there must be no swinging into the rider's outside leg. As the rider takes the forehand sideways and round, the horse must, if anything, step away from the outside leg of the rider.

At first the turn must be performed quite large so that the hind legs do keep on the move and the turn should be done slowly step by step to ensure control can be maintained.

Positioning insufficient

This means that the rider has failed to prepare the horse for a movement by not putting him into a position where he will be able to perform the exercise easily.

CORRECTION
Riders are not always fully aware of the difficulties the horse encounters if he is not in balance, or if his rider requires him to do something with too little warning.

Positioning mainly refers to the forehand and the control the rider has, or does not have, over it. The rider should be able to use the shoulder-in exercise to aid his control of the shoulders and the forehand, and if he is going to ride a corner or a circle he will use the shoulder-in position in a very minor degree to prepare the horse. In this way the shoulders do not fall out and the horse is more under control and better balanced.

Similarly, in canter it may be necessary to use a shoulder-in position to a minor degree to straighten the canter, if the quarters show signs of falling in. (For comments on the shoulder-in, see page 66.)

Preparation insufficient

This means that the rider has not warned the horse early enough of what is coming next and was probably unbalanced which may cause many other things to go wrong.

CORRECTION

Riders must know what they are about to do, and at what gait. This may sound obvious but many riders do not determine in their own minds exactly what they want to do so that they can prepare the horse.

The route and gait having been decided, the rider must warn the horse by some preparatory aids. If he is going forward, he should slightly increase the pressure of the aids for a second to gain the horse's attention.

If he wishes to slow down it may be necessary to use half halts to ensure that the balance is correct before trying the next exercise. This is applicable to all transitions if they are to be accurate at the markers.

Riders please note that if the horse has his head in the air, is crooked, or has too much or too little energy, he will not be able to do anything satisfactorily. These things must be put right before any attempt can be made to proceed to the next movement.

Quarters in or out

'Quarters out' means that instead of the hind legs following the forelegs as they should do, they are on a track to the outside of the forelegs. 'Quarters in' means the opposite; the hind legs are on a track to the inside of the forelegs. (See Figs. 11 and 12.)

CORRECTION

If the quarters fall out, the rider must first check that he is able to ride the horse on a straight line with the hind legs following the forelegs. Then he must achieve a correct bend with the hind legs still following the forelegs. This should be only a very slight bend at first and the outside leg is used against the horse to control any possible evasion. If the rider uses too much inside rein or allows more bend in the neck than the rest of his horse he will be encouraging the quarters to fall out, so this must be avoided.

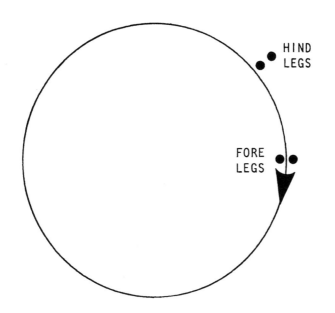

Fig. 11 Quarters out

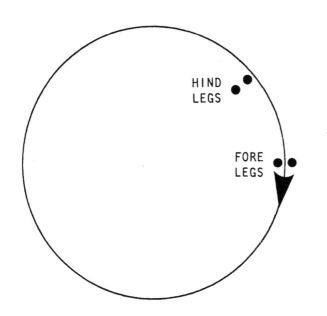

Fig. 12 Quarters in

The correction for quarters in is slightly different, it is usually necessary to use the shoulder-in exercise, to achieve the straightening.

It is a mistake to try to push the quarters out because this may cause swinging and many other problems. (For comments on the shoulder-in, see page 66.)

Quarters not engaged

This problem may not be easy to feel or to see unless the rider is fairly experienced. It means that, instead of the hind legs working under the horse, they are probably out behind, and there is insufficient flexion of the joints.

CORRECTION
The horse must be made to put his hind legs under him by first putting him at a speed where he cannot propel himself forward without bringing the hind legs under the body. This speed is usually quite slow and should be achieved by the use of half halts which will improve the balance so that the horse will carry himself.

Once the hind legs are in the right place the joints will automatically flex more and if asked for more activity by the use of the schooling whip, the quarters will then be doing their job effectively.

If the quarters are to be physically developed to their maximum strength, which they need to be to carry the horse through to advanced standard, the hind legs must be put in the right place from the start so that the horse may learn to carry himself in balance. (For comments on half halts, see page 12.)

Quarters leading or trailing

This comment refers to the half pass in which the horse should travel forwards and sideways, with his body, although he is bent in the direction he is going, remaining parallel to the side of the arena. On some occasions the quarters may be over too far, ahead of the forehand. In other instances the quarters will hardly be over at all and the horse is not crossing his hind legs. (See Figs. 13–15.)

CORRECTION
To teach the horse the half pass, the rider must first make sure he can take a flexion of the head and neck to one side or the other, keeping the remainder of the horse straight.

He must be able to come up the centre line with this

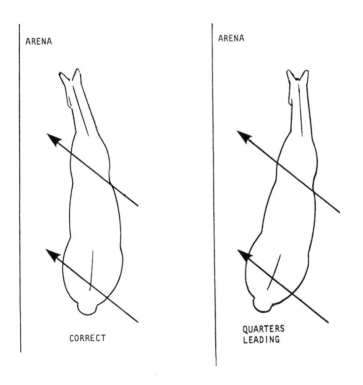

Fig. 13 Left half pass –
correct

Fig. 14 Left half pass –
quarters leading

flexion; when this is established he should draw his outside leg back, taking the forehand over with rein aids and controlling the quarters, asking them over as well. He must feel whether there is too much 'swing over' of the quarters to his leg, but if there is not enough reaction to his leg he must use the schooling whip to assist the leg.

When the horse goes sideways slowly under control, the rider may glance over his shoulder briefly to see where the quarters are, or someone on the ground can feed him information until he can feel what is happening for himself.

It is usually wise to begin in walk until the horse understands the aids.

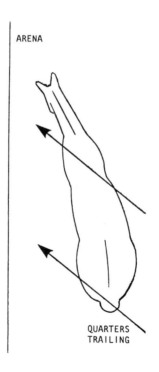

Fig. 15 Left half pass – quarters trailing

Quarters swinging

This means that the hindquarters are not under control between the rider's legs.

CORRECTION
During the horse's training he must be taught to accept a light even pressure from the rider's legs without taking his quarters from side to side in evasion. The rider must make sure that his horse does accept the legs and will go forward straight, from light aids. Even though the horse may dislike the feel of the legs against his sides, he will accept them in time, if the rider persists quietly.

Sometimes the quarters may get out of control because of having too much impulsion which cannot easily be controlled or because there is loss of balance.

The horse's quarters could also swing owing to resistance in the mouth.

The rider must first ascertain what the problem is and then carefully work on correcting it.

Quickened rather than extended

This comment ties in with *Running* and *Rushing* (see pages 94 and 95). It means that instead of the horse taking a longer stride in the same rhythm he probably goes onto the forehand and hurries along at a faster speed.

CORRECTION
When teaching the horse to extend, the rider should first teach some collection to properly engage the hindquarters. If the hind legs are under the horse and active, he will be able to push himself off into a longer stride which should have some elevation. The rider must allow the energy he has built up, by shortening or collecting the stride, to go forward but not 'down in front'. He must keep the balance level and, although not allowing the horse to lean, he must

expect rather a stronger contact due to increased impulsion.

Do not expect too much at first. The horse must gradually build up to his extension over a period of time. If too much is asked at first, the balance and rhythm will be lost.

The horse should 'offer' to go on a longer stride owing to the increase of energy in the quarters caused by the collection. The rider should take what is offered to begin with. Later, it may be necessary to tap the horse with the schooling whip to make him give more. (For comments on collection, see page 48.)

Rearing round

This term describes a horse which 'lifts' the forehand round, producing a canter pirouette in a slower tempo than the foregoing canter. The horse may come above the bit and, in addition, lose impulsion which might force the hind legs to pivot as the forehand labours to complete the turn.

CORRECTION
Keeping the correct sequence of canter together with a regular rhythm before, during and after the pirouette is important to its function. Lack of collection or insufficient impulsion will result in the horse labouring round the pirouette and may produce resistances. Impulsion must be maintained to ensure forward momentum; the horse must not 'sit back'. It is also wise to make the pirouette bigger rather than smaller until the horse's improved balance and collection enable him to cope with the smaller movement.

Rein-back crooked

In the rein-back, the steps should be even and straight and in two-time. One pair of diagonal legs and then the other.

When it is crooked, the quarters usually swing one way or the other and the strides will be uneven and, possibly, they will not be in two-time either.

CORRECTION
First, check on the mouth and the acceptance of the bit, if there is resistance to the hand, the quarters will inevitably swing.

When using the rein aids, the rider should aim at one step at a time, increasing the pressure on the mouth and then easing immediately the horse steps back.

If the horse puts his head in the air, or hollows his back, on no account attempt to rein-back because it is almost physically impossible. He must go back evenly between the rider's leg aids which should be light and even. Too much 'pushing' by the legs will hinder the horse and confuse him because he will think he is meant to go forward.

The rider may lean very slightly forward to allow the horse to use his back, which will come rounder as he steps back.

Concentrate on the straightness and ease of the movement.

(For comments on acceptance of the bit, see page 9).

Resisting

This term refers to any desire from the horse to evade his rider's aids. For example, he may open his mouth, cross his jaw, put his tongue out, tilt his head, swing his quarters, kick to the leg or just plain nap.

CORRECTION
If the evasion is in the mouth the improvement must be made by correcting the acceptance of the bit. Once the horse is 'giving' in his jaw the rider should be able to overcome the resistance.

If the horse is evading the legs aids, the rider must first pay attention to whether the horse is going forwards willingly to a light aid. If not, he must use the schooling whip, to assist the leg. If necessary the whip may have to be applied quite firmly at first, until the horse respects it and will then go forward from a light tap.

If he kicks to the leg, the stick should be used immediately after each kick until it stops. Many riders do not follow this through thinking that the more they use the stick the more the horse kicks. However, if this resistance is to be overcome, the rider must persist with the stick until the horse will accept the feel of it being applied.

Napping of course can be a great problem especially if allowed to become confirmed.

The rider should be very careful not to allow the young horse to find out his own strength. He should be guided firmly but with care to the rider's wishes, which if taught properly should cause no problem. However, mistakes are made and if the same mistake is made too often the horse will soon take advantage.

It is a mistake to think that you cannot be really firm with the young horse. He must know that when the rider wishes to go forward, he must go, and when asked to accept the bit he must do so. This should be the rider's first job. It should not be left as it so often is, with the horse being ridden on a loose rein for several months. He then learns to go that way and when the rider takes a contact he usually objects.

With the spoilt older horse, it is much more complicated to overcome nappiness or resistance and expert help may be needed. The best advice I can give is to go back to the beginning and start again! Treat the horse as a youngster and go through the basic programme making the correction as and when required.

The rider must bear in mind that if a horse has been ridden incorrectly for years, all his muscles and his physique may be developed incorrectly and it will take great patience and much riding of the school exercises to soften the hard muscles, so that the horse is able to change his way of going.

He may not be resisting because he is a pig but simply because he has been badly ridden, and the rider will have to use all his intelligence and knowledge of the correct basic training to enable the changes to take place. (For comments on the acceptance of the bit, see page 9.)

Resting leg

Applies to the halt where the horse should be taking an even weight on all four legs. In this instance he may be resting one leg and only standing on three.

CORRECTION
The rider must bring the horse to the halt in a balanced manner so that the weight is evenly distributed.

If the rider takes his legs away from the horse at the halt which makes him feel unsupported, it gives him the opportunity to rest a leg.

During training the rider must ensure that the hocks are coming under the horse in the halt, and that they are not left behind. If the quarters are not engaged, it will be more difficult to keep the legs under control.

Restricted

Restricted means that the rider has for one reason or another held the gait back so that it is too slow, or he may cause the stride to be too short so that the horse cannot use himself.

CORRECTION
Restriction often occurs because the horse is pulling or trying to go too fast and the rider tries to keep him under control with the hands only. Usually the horse will become slower without engaging the hindquarters. He may become overbent and shorten his stride so that he hardly puts one foot in front of the other.

The rider must endeavour to gain control over the speed

by using half halts and when the horse is better balanced and going on a lighter rein, he will then be more relaxed. With the relaxation comes a longer stride. The rider must then concentrate on the rhythm and keeping the horse light on the hand.

Rough transition. See *Transition rough*, page 104.

Running

This term is usually used when the horse is dashing along too fast on the forehand, with no balance or rhythm and very little suspension in the stride.

CORRECTION. See *Rushing*, page 95.

Rushed back

This refers to the rein-back when the horse, instead of listening to the rider's aids, takes it upon himself to go back at the speed of his choosing.

CORRECTION
The horse can only rush back if the rider permits it, and, if this is happening, then the aids and control over the horse are at fault.

At all times the horse should be in front of the rider's leg (see page 17) so that if the rider wishes the horse to go forwards he is in a position to make that happen. When teaching rein-back, it is advisable to try to obtain a step at a time so that any inclination to rush is checked. Also, keeping the poll as the highest point of the forehand prevents the horse ducking his head and evading the control in that way.

Rushing

This generally means that the gait is too hurried and that there is a lack of balance and rhythm.

CORRECTION
The rider is in control of the gait, or should be, and it is up to him to know when his horse is balanced and to keep the gait steady.

Some horses are more impetuous than others and do want to surge forwards or keep increasing the speed. The rider must use the half halts to achieve greater control over the gaits and if the horse learns to carry himself in balance he will find it much easier not to rush.

If constantly reminded in the beginning, horses will learn to go at a particular speed at each gait and will not expect to go faster all the time. The rider is responsible for teaching this to the horse.

In no way must the rider hang on to the horse's head to slow him down. This may cause the horse to pull against the rider. If the half halts are used correctly this should not happen.

The rider must always be aware of the rhythm of the footfalls in the various gaits so that he can regulate the strides. (For additional comments on half halts and balance, see pages 12 and 15.)

Shoulders falling out

This term indicates that the rider has lost control of the forehand and is allowing the horse's shoulders to break the true line of the curve, or the straight line.

CORRECTION
The rider must be well aware of the use of his outside rein and leg when riding a curve.

He must avoid too much bend in the neck which will give

a false curve and allow the shoulders to fall out.

He should ask for the bend with the inside rein and leg, but then control the amount with the outside rein and leg. He should aim at being able to ride a curve with the outside rein and inside leg, with a *very* light inside rein contact.

He must make sure that the horse is not deviating from the correct line of the curve as shown. (See Figs. 16–18.)

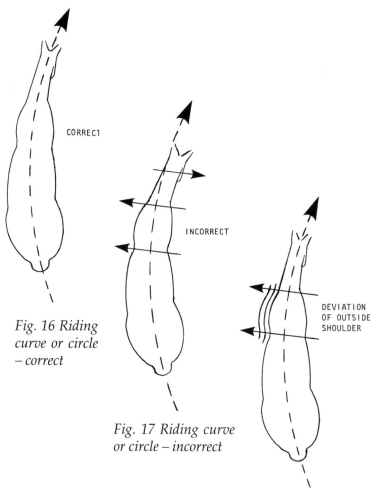

Fig. 16 Riding curve or circle – correct

Fig. 17 Riding curve or circle – incorrect

Fig. 18 Deviation of outside shoulder

Stiff

This comment occurs so often and means that whereas the horse should curve round a circle or a corner, he moves without bend or even flexion.

CORRECTION
To move efficiently the horse must become supple in his back and must curve his whole length on a circle or part of a circle, a corner etc.

First the rider must see whether he can produce a small head flexion to one side and then the other. The rider should feel one side of the mouth and turn the horse's head very slightly to the same side. If the horse yields to the hand, then the rider may try the other side.

If all is well and the horse is even in his mouth, the rider should use the rein to achieve the flexion and then his leg to encourage some 'give' under the saddle. If the horse is dead to the leg, use the schooling whip to achieve the result. When the leg is applied the horse must offer to move away from it. Then the outside rein and leg must 'catch' him and control the bend and make sure he is keeping to the line of the circle, etc.

Subsequently, the shoulder-in exercise must be taught to increase the control of the forehand and make the muscles more supple by the increased bend and activity of the inside hind leg. (For comments on shoulder-in, see page 00.)

Strike-off late or early

The canter did not start at the marker.

CORRECTION
In training the rider will put his young horse, or a disobedient older horse, into canter on a corner, to help him strike off on the correct leg.

When this is understood by the horse, the rider must

begin to make the strike-off in other places and then, finally, at a precise point. He must make the horse very obedient to the lightest of aids so that with only a minimum of preparation he can ask for complete obedience and get the strike-off where he wants it.

The schooling whip may have to be employed to achieve the obedience, but once the horse understands, it can be dispensed with.

Stuck

This comment refers to a walk pirouette when one or more steps have become stationary or pivoted.

CORRECTION

A correct pirouette can only take place if the preceding walk steps are sufficiently collected and active. Riders sometimes avoid the collection for fear of losing the correct sequence of steps or because they may cause a break in the gait, but if the horse is truly accepting the aids, allowing himself to be properly engaged, these problems should not occur. Pirouettes often become stuck because the rider has allowed the horse to drop impulsion (see page 43) when the turn begins instead of trying to maintain the tempo of the collected walk during the turn.

Swishing tail

Some horses will swish their tails during a test in an angry and resistant fashion; some may momentarily swing the tail occasionally. In either case it may be classed as resistance and marked down in the submission section.

CORRECTION

Most horses swish their tails because they find a certain movement difficult.

If they are trained correctly, with careful preparation and proper relaxation, the difficulties should not occur. With systematic physical development there will not be any reason to show resistance by tail swishing.

The horse must accept the rider's aids, particularly the legs. If there is hesitation it is preferable to use the schooling whip to overcome it at the start than to wait and have trouble later.

With an older horse, the problem will be difficult to stamp out, but the rider should pay attention to correcting the acceptance of the leg aids.

When the horse is using his back correctly, the tail will swing from side to side in rhythm with the strides and will show no sign of stiffness in the dock.

Some tail swishing may be due to stiffness in the back and if the horse is made more supple it may then cease.

A suppling exercise which may help is the shoulder-in, (see page 66.)

Swung round

This comment is made with reference to a pirouette in walk or canter when the horse has possibly turned on the centre, or made the turn too fast and not under control.

With the canter pirouette, the strides of the canter may be lost and the horse will swing or pivot on one or both hind legs.

CORRECTION

Control over the stride is the important factor. The horse must not be allowed to turn at his own speed but to come round stride by stride. The strides must be of even size.

In the walk the four-time gait must be maintained and when teaching the turn, the horse should be asked to go one step and then halt, until he has completed the turn. The rider can then control the steps and prevent the horse walking forwards or backwards. Also he can make sure that the quarters do not swing into the outside leg. He must lead the forehand round with his reins used equally, (not more pressure on the inside) easing the hand between each step. There should be a slight flexion to the way he is turning.

As soon as the horse understands the aids he must be asked to do the turn in walk and the hind legs will be expected to be mobile, rather like marching on the spot. First, a semi-collected walk must be achieved so that the horse can turn almost on the same spot. Later, when the horse is in real collection, the turn *must* be completely on the spot.

In canter the sequence of the steps (see page 30) must be maintained. The horse must canter in the turn, not rear round or fling himself sideways.

First, a very collected canter must be achieved so that the horse can remain in balance almost on the spot, on the straight line, then he must bend in the direction of the turn. Only when these things are correct can the rider ask for the turn. The aids are the same as for the walk turn, with the inside leg maintaining the canter.

Usually in the half turn, four strides are asked for, and in a full turn, eight. The same number of strides should be shown in the left pirouette as in the right.

Tense

This term describes the state of the horse both mentally and physically, when he is worked up either by outside distractions, or because he has not been taught to relax.

CORRECTION
It is necessary for the horse to be mentally calm if he is to learn and remember what is being taught.

He will be receptive only when he is mentally and physically relaxed. Stiff, tense muscles cannot comply easily to the rider's aids.

How do you achieve this especially when some horses are much more lively than others? Speed is one bugbear of the tense horse. Usually he is too impulsive, so it is necessary to remove this by going very slowly, until the horse realises there is nothing to be excited about. Work on a large circle, in a steady trot; using half halts generally helps the horse to become quieter and less tense.

It may take longer to calm the canter, but work on the trot will eventually improve the whole situation. (For comments on half halts, see page 12.)

Tipping or tilting head

This states that the face of the horse is not held vertically. From the front, the head is slanted to the right or to the left. (See Fig. 19.)

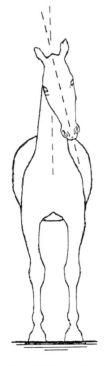

Fig. 19 Head tilted

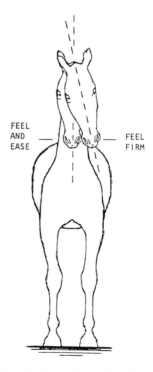

Fig. 20 Correcting tilted head

CORRECTION

If the rider has trained his horse to go straight from the beginning, this problem should not occur. However, mistakes are made and sometimes some tilting will occur, very often when the rider is trying to achieve a bend in half pass for instance.

To correct this it will be necessary to go back to the beginning and to try to obtain the straightness, paying great attention to the head and neck, and the evenness of the acceptance of the hands.

If there is difficulty the rider may keep the feel firm on the side to which the nose is tilting, then feel and ease the hand on the other side to encourage the head to come straight. (See Fig. 20.)

Tongue back

Some horses evade the bit by drawing their tongues back into their mouths so that the bit is not pressing on it. Any evasion of this kind is unacceptable and will be marked down.

CORRECTION

Teaching the horse to accept the bit readily is crucial to the training and needs to be taught by a skilled rider. Many riders fail in this respect because of ignorance, lack of sympathy and bad hands, causing the horse to evade in all manner of ways. A thorough knowledge of how to 'make a mouth' is needed so that faults never arise. Once they do, they are often difficult or impossible to correct. Remaking the mouth of a spoilt horse needs an expert, a kind bit and plenty of patience to regain the horse's confidence. The rider will need the ability to use a squeezing contact to obtain a yielding by the mouth to bit pressure, which, when it occurs, must be rewarded by a lightening of the contact. This can only happen if the horse is ridden forward from the leg aids and can take a considerable time to achieve.

Tongue out

Sometimes the horse will put his tongue out of the side of his mouth. It may be for a moment, or he may do it continuously. Either way it is an evasion of the bit.

Because the horse is not accepting the correct influence of the bit he will be severely penalised.

CORRECTION
The rider should first make sure that there is nothing wrong with the bit, i.e. too severe, worn, pinching, etc.

He should then ensure that his hands are not causing the horse discomfort by having a too strong and unsympathetic contact. If these points are not a problem he should try to work on the acceptance of the bit.

It may also be worth having the teeth checked in case they are sharp. (For comments on the acceptance of bit, see page 9.)

Tongue over the bit

This is an evasion whereby the horse puts his tongue over the top of the bit instead of keeping it underneath thus getting away from the correct influence of the bit.

CORRECTION
Because the influence of the bit is lost if the tongue is put over it, the rider must do all he can to prevent this habit occuring in the first place.

Young horses sometimes develop the habit as the result of being left in the stable tacked up. They start to play around with the bit which is still strange to them and discover that it is more comfortable or more entertaining to alter the tongue position; therefore it may be unwise to put the horse in this situation.

An older horse may merely have discovered that he can be less easily controlled by putting the tongue over the mouthpiece, so will do this whenever he wishes to evade the aids. The rider must try to achieve a better acceptance of the bit and employ the use of a correctly fitted drop noseband to prevent the horse opening his mouth. (For comments on the acceptance of the bit, see page 9.)

Too low

This is really the same as being on the forehand and means that the whole front of the horse is carrying too much weight.

CORRECTION. See *On the forehand*, page 77.

Transition not defined

The transitions, as stated previously, must be performed at the designated marker.

It is sometimes required that there should be a change of gait from medium to collected canter. This change is also a transition and as such should show a distinct difference.

If the horse is allowed to drift from one gait to the other the transition will hardly be seen and may be described as not defined.

CORRECTION. See *Not enough difference*, page 68.

Transition rough

During a test there are many transitions, or changes, from one gait to another. These should be smooth, straight and balanced. Any resistance to the hand will make a transition rough.

CORRECTION

The rider should know exactly where he wants to make a transition, so that he can prepare the horse sufficiently.

The horse must be straight and not going too fast or he will be uncontrolled. He must be in balance and the rider may use half halts to achieve this state.

The rider must prepare the horse by a couple of warning aids to make sure he is attentive and then, as the horse's head comes level with the marker, he should ask for the transition, which should happen, smoothly and with no alteration of the head position, by the time the rider's leg reaches the marker.

The canter to trot transition always causes difficulty at first because the weight of the horse often falls forward and the rider will tip onto the shoulders. The rider must endeavour to balance the canter and shorten the strides before the transition. As soon as the horse breaks, the rider must sit up as steadily as possible and immediately correct the surging trot speed.

Once the horse has learned that he may not race forwards in trot he will gradually steady himself in the trot providing the preparation in canter has been attended to. If the hand is not accepted the horse will probably throw his head up or down which will also make the transition rough, so the rider should make sure that the horse will give to the bit when extra contact is taken. (For additional comments on the acceptance of the bit and half halts, see pages 9 and 12.)

Tripped

This means that during a movement the horse tripped in one or more strides.

CORRECTION

The main cause of tripping is usually lack of, or loss of, balance.

Marks will be lost for persistent tripping because it shows

lack of balance, but if it is only a momentary mistake in the case of a young horse, the judge will probably be quite lenient, as long as it does not affect the movement too much.

Some horses trip when they are fatigued, or, if young, because they cannot organise their weight and that of their riders, very well.

The rider must make it as easy as possible for the horse to carry himself and his rider by sitting as still as possible and preventing the horse getting onto the forehand.

The horse's feet should be checked because excessively long toes can cause tripping.

Turn on centre

This comment applies to a pirouette when the horse fails to keep the hindquarters on the spot. The rider allows the horse to swing his quarters against the outside leg instead of keeping them still.

CORRECTION. See *Swung round*, page 99.

Unbalanced

This remark describes the state of the horse when he has lost his balance temporarily or completely.

If the balance is good in the first place and the horse becomes unbalanced only for a moment, he will probably be able to regain it again quite soon and so will not lose many marks.

If, however, the balance was not very good in the first place, the horse may experience difficulty in trying to perform several movements, and may fall on the forehand to the degree that the rider will be unable to regain control.

Some horses will go through the whole test in an unbalanced manner. Many marks will be forfeited in this case.

CORRECTION
The rider must learn about balance because it is up to him to put the weight in the right place. Some horses are naturally well balanced and others are not but, whatever the situation is, the rider must help the horse by distributing the weight evenly. (For comments on balance, see page 15.)

Uneven steps

Uneven steps may occur in any movement, but the term is mainly used with reference to passage and piaffe.

CORRECTION
Where even steps are not maintained, the fault lies in loss of engagement or impulsion. At all times, it is up to the rider to be in control of the energy and to be able to regulate it so that evenness and regularity are maintained.

Unlevel

This is a reference to the strides of the horse and may be seen in walk and particularly in trot.

It means, for example, that instead of the front feet taking even weight as they come to the ground, one may be taking more than the other, giving the appearance of slight lameness.

The strides may also be uneven, one leg coming further forward than the other.

All this also applies to the hind legs and, in addition, one hock may come higher than the other.

CORRECTION
Unlevelness can be caused in several ways. Firstly, any unevenness in the acceptance of the bit can cause the horse to be unlevel or 'bridle lame'.

Secondly, if the physical development of the horse is

uneven it will cause one-sidedness.

Most horses have a hollow side so the rider has to try to stretch the muscles on that side in order to make the horse straight. He does this by using the school movements, circles, serpentines etc. and suppling exercises such as shoulder-in.

It is important to ride straight lines as well as circles to make sure that the horse is working evenly. Should the muscles on one side be stronger than the other the horse will find it easier to push off harder with the strong hind leg. The weaker one may lag behind which will make the horse unlevel.

Riding on only one diagonal can cause uneven steps, so it is important to change the diagonal when changing the rein.

Riders must not expect drastic changes to take place; the horse will only even up over a period of time with patient and systematic work.

Unsteady halt

This comment is used when the horse comes to the halt but does not really achieve immobility. He may fidget with his legs, or his head, or move off the line.

CORRECTION. See *Moved at halt*, page 59.

Unsteady head

This remark describes the lack of steadiness in the head carriage.

Some horses may be unsteady in their head carriage throughout the test.

Some may be unsteady for a moment due to a loss of balance while executing a difficult movement.

CORRECTION

A steady head carriage is only achieved by good balance and the correct acceptance of the bit (see page 9.) Balance must be maintained by the rider if the horse is to be able to control his neck and head, which he uses to balance himself naturally. By working at the correct speed and in rhythm, any movement the horse needs to make will be minimal and so the rider is able to ask him to keep his head still.

In walk, the head and neck must be allowed to move up and down a little, this is necessary for the action of the walk strides.

In trot, the head and neck are less active and there should be a consistent position with relatively no movement.

In canter, owing to the action of the canter strides, the horse will be allowed some movement of the neck up and down but the head should be still with the nose vertical or slightly in front of the vertical. (See Fig. 21.)

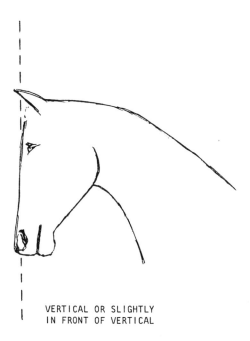

VERTICAL OR SLIGHTLY
IN FRONT OF VERTICAL

Fig. 21 Head still – nose vertical

Wandering

This term is usually used when the horse has deviated from the straight line or circle on which he started, i.e. if he is following the line of a 20 m circle and he makes the circle larger or smaller for a moment, he could be said to be wandering.

CORRECTION
If the horse wanders it is usually the fault of the rider who has failed to keep him between the hand and leg and has allowed him to come off the aids.

If the horse is being made to go forward from the rider's leg aids and is kept at a steady speed, he should have enough energy to go forward into the bridle. If this is so, the rider will be able to keep a good contact with a steady rein encouraging the horse to go forward and straight. The horse's strides should then be purposeful.

If the rider is decisive in his directions, the horse will understand what is required and will be less likely to wander about.

Wrong bend

Many riders fail to achieve the correct bend of the horse in the corners, circles etc. The horse should be slightly curved in the direction he is going. If this is incorrect many marks will be lost not only for wrong bend, but also for the resulting problems, such as lack of balance, rhythm, etc.

CORRECTION
The rider should first make sure that he can ride straight with even acceptance of the bit and leg aids. He should then try to make the horse flex to one hand and then the other. This should be very slight and is only done to check on the 'give' of each side of the mouth. The horse must also yield to the leg when it is applied. The schooling whip can be used to help achieve this.

Once the horse gives to the hand and leg, a bend can be achieved. The horse must be bent uniformly from nose to tail, with no more bend in the neck than the rest of the horse. Because the horse cannot physically bend his spine very much the bend is quite slight.

The rider must be able to change the bend from one rein to the other but, because the horse needs time to organise himself, the rider must prepare for the change of bend by riding straight for a few strides. The horse must accept a small flexion to the new direction on the straight before he is allowed to go round on the new rein.

Consideration must also be given to the outside leg of the rider which has to control the quarters and keep the bend round the inside leg. A true bend will not be achieved without this acceptance.

Wrong leg not corrected

This comment is used when the rider has allowed the horse to strike off in the canter with the wrong leading leg and does not correct it before the movement finishes. In this case the judge will probably give no marks for that movement.

CORRECTION
When cantering normally round the arena, the horse should lead with the inside foreleg, followed by the inside hind leg, and he should be bent in the direction he is going.

With the young or difficult horse, it will be as well to start in a corner with the horse straight, no flexion to either hand particularly. He may need to lengthen the trot strides a little at first, but soon he must answer the leg aids which can be backed up by the schooling whip held in the outside hand.

If there is any deviation from the track to the outside, the horse will almost certainly strike off wrong. If wishing to strike off to the right, for example, the rider should feel that the balance is a little to the right, but definitely not to the left. He must control the horse with his outside rein and leg.

He may use the schooling whip against the outside shoulder if the horse persists in trying to go towards the outside of the track.

Too much bend in the neck will hinder the horse and this should be avoided.

The rider must learn to feel which foreleg is coming forward in the strike-off so that he knows before the canter really starts which leg the horse will be on. If the horse fails to make the correct strike-off the rider must bring him back to trot quickly, check the balance and try again.